Praise for
WORTHY

"*Worthy* is like an oasis in the desert known as poverty, despair, and unlovingness. It illuminates the part of each of us that was taught a lie. A lie that tells us we're not worthy and lovable just as we are. Read *Worthy*. And as you do, allow those layers of shame, guilt, and unlovingness to melt away. Then watch what happens with your finances. Bravo Nancy Levin . . . this book is a treasure."

— Christiane Northrup, M.D., *New York Times* best-selling author of *Goddesses Never Age*

"We're telling ourselves the wrong story—money is not the issue. When we think we're unworthy, we believe we have to prove that we have a right to prosperity. If you're not holding yourself, within yourself, as worthy, abundance won't be able to penetrate your consciousness. In her powerful book *Worthy*, Nancy Levin links fears and limitations surrounding resources to low self-esteem and seeking external validation. Worthiness is an inside job. Let *Worthy* be your guide to self-honoring transformation in service of the life you desire and deserve."

— Iyanla Vanzant, *New York Times* best-selling author and host of *Iyanla Fix My Life* on *OWN*

"It's easy to attach our self-worth to our money issues. But when we do, we unknowingly block the abundance all around us. Luckily, Nancy Levin is changing this broken dynamic in her new book, *Worthy*. In it she walks us through a simple process to unravel the money knots that keep us bound and unprosperous. With practical exercises and relatable tales, *Worthy* will leave you feeling inspired to create the life you want to live—one that includes emotional freedom around money."

r, *New York Times* best-selling author of *Crazy Sexy Juice*

"Abundance begins with your mind-set. If you think lacking thoughts, that lack will be reflected in your bank account. In *Worthy*, Nancy Levin provides the very key you need to start cleaning up your thoughts and energy around money—right now. Energy is currency and when your energy has an essence of prosperity, you greatly increase your capacity to receive even more. Let Nancy show you how to open your mind-set to all you deserve in service of raising your self-worth and your net worth."

— Gabrielle Bernstein, *New York Times* best-selling author of *Miracles Now*

"Nancy Levin writes from her heart, revealing at a fundamental level who we really are and what we're really worth."

— Marianne Williamson, *New York Times* best-selling author of *Tears to Triumph*

"*Worthy* is a beautifully deep dive into what money is really about. If you want to make headway in your financial life, this book will be a wise and fruitful guide. It won't be what you expect but I bet it will be what you need."

— Kate Northrup, *New York Times* best-selling author of *Money: A Love Story*

"Low self-worth isn't just a cloud on our self-esteem, it darkens our entire well-being, including our financial sustainability. My fierce friend Nancy Levin guides us clearly to ignite massive healing of how we feel about ourselves and clear all the quirky, self-destructive habits that hold us back from our full potential. Worthy gives us a path out of fear and into sunny abundance."

— Tara Stiles, founder of Strala Yoga

"I just love this work by Nancy Levin! It's so important and long overdue! So many of us who work in the spiritual/ self-help genre have bought into the myth that 'money is not spiritual.' However, this falsely held belief has propagated a culture of people who truly have trouble receiving and giving money for work that comes from the heart. Nancy's book really hits home the fact that if we love ourselves, that means not only taking care of our mind, body, and spirit, but it also includes taking care of our finances as well. Thank you, Nancy, for writing a book that truly integrates conscious awareness with financial awareness, and how our value of ourselves can affect our financial worth. I will be referring this book to a lot of people!"

— Anita Moorjani, *New York Times*
best-selling author of *Dying to Be Me*

"For everyone who recognizes that their money issues are connected to self-esteem, this is the book you need to read. In my opinion, healthy self-esteem conquers money issues more successfully than financial courses any day."

— Caroline Myss, *New York Times* best-selling author
of *Anatomy of the Spirit* and *Defy Gravity*

"With a patient hand and a loving touch, Nancy Levin guides us to discover our inner worth and thus multiply our outer wealth! A must-read if you're looking to improve your financial future, while finding the inner peace, passion, and purpose we all long for."

— Nick Ortner, *New York Times* best-selling
author of *The Tapping Solution*

"For most of us, addressing challenges with money feels overwhelming, and books about the topic, just as overwhelming. Finally, with *Worthy*, Nancy Levin delivers the compassion and hand-holding advice to help you take steps forward in a way that feels easy and even fun. Start here to improve your finances and you'll improve your whole life in the process."

— Jessica Ortner, *New York Times* best-selling author of *The Tapping Solution for Weight Loss and Body Confidence*

"Nancy Levin's book *Worthy* is a real gem. I love the way she dives deep into the inner work revealing that our thoughts, beliefs, feelings, and early decisions about money all contribute to our current level of wealth. For anyone who's having trouble with money, this is a must-read."

— Barbara Stanny, *New York Times* best-selling author of *Overcoming Underearning* and *Sacred Success*

"*Worthy* is a wonderful book that instantly propels you into the source of how to activate soaring abundance, while also holding the keys to soaring self-esteem. Highly recommended!"

— Denise Linn, author of *Kindling the Native Spirit*

Testimonials for
WORTHY

"I can honestly say that Nancy Levin's Worthy Coaching was the best 'spiritual business decision' I ever made! Parts of me that were spiritually dormant for years were awakened, and finances that I once feared looking at were faced. Once they were exposed, there was no turning back to the person I was pre-Worthy Coaching. This coaching changed me on a cellular level and cemented in me a deep knowing that I can accomplish anything. I've found a self-love quite like nothing else I've ever experienced. I know my boundaries. I know the difference between rescuing or people pleasing and offering help or support. I've learned clear self-nourishing practices to remind myself I'm worth taking an extra five minutes for. I've learned to say no and be okay with it. Worthy Coaching is gold. Each session opens up new beliefs and practices to keep myself grounded, alive, adventurous, and worthy of the greatest life I can create. I am eternally grateful."

— Cathy Anello, a Worthy Coaching client

"I was vacillating on the amount of money to ask my boss for in a raise. Nancy coached me to the place I felt aligned and worthy. I was able to confidently ask for and receive a $30,000 raise!!! I'm soooo incredibly grateful for Nancy and her coaching process. I KNOW I am Worthy."

— Julie Jacky, Certified EFT Practitioner

"As a result of the Worthy Coaching my business has grown, I have more confidence in the work I am doing. I have more communication about money with my spouse. I have a heightened awareness of my own patterns and programs and have come to really understand that worthiness is an internal job and does not come from anything outside of me."

— Barb Klein

"I'm so much more alive and in touch with who I am and what I want. I am recognizing lots of opportunities to set appropriate boundaries. I'm moving forward one step at a time towards a future that I once thought was only reserved for fairy-tale endings. And I started a business and am getting paid for it! Woo hoo! I never would have imagined that a new business would be a result of our Worthy Coaching, and I am so excited about it!"

— Dorena Kohrs

"Prior to Worthy Coaching, I thought the only way to feel freedom was to be financially free. During the coaching, I realized it's up to me to create that feeling of freedom regardless of my bank account. I learned that my net worth equated to how I felt mentally, emotionally, spiritually, and physically—where I used to think of it only in terms of finances. Since the first class, my whole life and schedule has changed. I'm now homeschooling my daughter; I'm reconnected with my partner; I sleep in more; I rest more; I have a lot more creative energy; I'm working on my business; I'm taking time to heal my body from a physical trauma; I have all the time I need to do whatever I need. THIS is freedom, and it came without paying off my house, which is what I used to tie "freedom" to. Though it's still a goal to be financially free, I feel more able to accomplish it because I'm living life on my terms. This coaching module is fabulous and Nancy is genius! I'm a rich woman!"

— Christine Gipple

"Nancy Levin is a gift! With her experience and insight, she guided me through the Worthy Coaching steps that changed not only my bank accounts, but my attitude about what I deserve."

— Barb Ridener, PhD

"As a result of Worthy Coaching, I've taken my power back in all ways—physically, mentally, emotionally, and financially. I feel empowered and believe in myself and my capabilities on my own!"

— Sarah Grace

"Here's what I did as a result of my Worthy Coaching: I called companies to get money credited back to me that I did not owe. Reconciled my accounts. Paid off higher credit cards. Put all my accounts in my name only so that I would know the exact amount in each account and be able to transfer and manage them myself. Stopped giving away and discounting my services."

— Sandy Picard

WORTHY

WORTHY

BOOST YOUR SELF-WORTH
TO GROW YOUR NET WORTH

NANCY LEVIN

Author of Jump . . . And Your Life Will Appear

HAY HOUSE, INC.
Carlsbad, California • New York City
London • Sydney • Johannesburg
Vancouver • New Delhi

Published and distributed in the United States by: Hay House, Inc.: www
.hayhouse.com® • *Published and distributed in Australia by:* Hay House
Australia Pty. Ltd.: www.hayhouse.com.au • *Published and distributed
in the United Kingdom by:* Hay House UK, Ltd.: www.hayhouse.co.uk •
Published and distributed in the Republic of South Africa by: Hay House
SA (Pty), Ltd.: info@hayhouse.co.za • *Distributed in Canada by:* Raincoast
Books: www.raincoast.com • *Published in India by:* Hay House Publishers
India: www.hayhouse.co.in

Cover design: Charles McStravick • *Interior design:* Tricia Breidenthal

Cataloging-in-Publication Data is on file at the Library of Congress

Tradepaper ISBN: 978-1-4019-5015-6

10 9 8 7 6 5 4 3 2 1
1st edition, August 2016

Printed in the United States of America

CONTENTS

WHOLE

while the healing navigates
the map my heart and mind makes
it's the radiating rhythm
of vibration and stillness
that now allows me
to receive what hides
and translate all there is to see

this journey to knowing
deep in my essence
that i am loved
no matter what i do or don't do
even if i don't do *anything* i will be loved

but to believe, i needed courage
i found it in my body

my body
a treasure chest
its cellular secrets under lock and key
until the moment they were ready to be freed

knowing my worth
is inside of me,
it can't be given
or taken away

my power is very confusing
and although my legs just want to run
i can feel my feet begin to find their roots
sourcing safety for my strength

the thaw begins like this
after being frozen in place
for so long
waves of flame and prayer
release me
finally locating the passage
from my heart
revealing the way to healing

and so in the softening
i learn that love
presents in many forms

my thoughts
my own
for the first time

and as pieces of me
return or arrive
desire alone senses
the rise and fall
of what's alive
inside

now
stripped of all
i once defined
myself by
it takes only a moment
to notice
i have always been
worthy
i have always been
whole

FOREWORD

How much is your time, energy, love, and hard work worth? If this question makes you cringe, then this book is for you. Self-worth is a dynamic of emotional and mental health that is sadly neglected.

After all, unless you value yourself, you won't have the motivation to exercise, get enough sleep, eat healthfully, and care for yourself. As I wrote about in my book *Don't Let Anything Dull Your Sparkle*, many of us have suffered from traumatic experiences that have shattered our sense of safety, self-worth, and inner peace. Unless we learn to value ourselves, we won't ask for what we need, and we won't accept help when it's offered. Those who've been traumatized often view other people as more deserving.

As someone who has studied, lived, and helped to treat co-dependency for many decades, I see too many loving and gentle people giving endlessly to other people. They give away their time, money, love, and help to those who only take and never return anything. Being generous is an admirable trait, but only if it is balanced with being generous toward your own self. And when you value yourself, you become more discerning about *whom* you give your time and love to.

One thing I've learned is that both giving and receiving are equally important and necessary. We must inhale *and* exhale in order to live. The same is true with our finances as well.

Nancy and I have known each other as work associates and friends for many years. We both had similar marriages to men whom we financially supported. We also got divorced at the same time, and gave each other comfort and support as our ex-husbands pursued and received alimony and large settlements. Those experiences made us stronger.

Mostly, though, Nancy and I both learned that self-care is much more than taking the time for meditation, yoga, and healthful eating. Self-care means taking care of your financial life, too! That's why I'm so happy that Nancy has gathered the wisdom you'll need for financial self-care in her new book, *Worthy*. In this book are hard-won lessons that Nancy is gifting to you, because she doesn't want you to repeat the painful lessons that she and I endured. If you'll take her messages to heart, and apply them to your life, you will prevent needless stress and also ensure that you have the resources you need.

Many people on the spiritual path have difficulty facing their finances, because money is viewed as materialistic, shallow, and low-vibrating. Well, money *can* be those things when used in the service of the ego.

But money can also be used in the service of the Divine. When you have financial security, you have the wherewithal to open your own business, take time for your life purpose, buy organic food, and give donations to your favorite charities. As much as we may resent the whole financial system, it is the way that earth life works at this time. We can fight it, or we can learn how to work with money to make the world a better place.

Money is a metaphor for abundance and feeling like you have enough in life. I've met plenty of wealthy people who are still financially insecure. It's not how much you have, but feeling like you have enough, that matters the most.

When we claim our worthiness and start valuing our time, finances, and happiness, then we are open to receiving abundance in all forms. We realize that it's safe to have free time, fun, love, and all the other pleasures of life. We no

longer apologize for our success, and we let our lights shine brightly to inspire others.

My prayer is that you'll read this entire book and complete the written exercises Nancy has provided for you. You'll be amazed at how much stronger you feel!

With love and respect,

Doreen

Doreen Virtue, author of *The Courage to be Creative, Don't Let Anything Dull Your Sparkle,* and *Angels of Abundance*

INTRODUCTION

Why Personal Finance Books Don't Work . . . But This One Will

Money. We love it. We hate it. We want more of it. We wish we didn't need it. For many of us, it's a constant source of anxiety . . . and arguments with our loved ones. If we don't have much money, we're struggling to get more. If we do have money, we're struggling to figure out how to keep it. And then, how to manage it.

Does money have to be such a source of anxiety? No! Can our relationship with it be less complicated? Yes! How am I so sure? Because I've lived it. I've worked through a lot of dysfunction about money and come out the other side. And I've helped many others resolve crippling issues with money as well.

Maybe you're dealing with some of the same issues, and you're stuck in a pattern like one of these:

- You're scared of financial ruin, so you avoid looking at your credit card bills or reconciling your bank statements.

- You're staying in an unhappy relationship because you're afraid you can't support yourself.

- You're racking up debt, and you're worried you'll never be able to pay it off.

- You make enough money to get by, but you can't seem to save any.

- You have money, but you feel uncomfortable and afraid to spend it. No amount ever feels like enough.

Or any number of other scenarios . . .

In other words, if you're reading this book,
there's something up in your relationship with money.

Maybe you've read all the (many) financial books out there. They make sense to you, but they don't seem to *work for you.*

What's the problem?

Let me explain. The issue with most financial books is that they teach you how to change what you *do* with your money. They give you advice about how and where to invest, how the stock market works, how to get out of credit card debt, and how to tell the difference between the various types of funds and trusts.

The real key to creating financial freedom isn't about changing what you *do.* It's about changing how you *feel.* And that requires more than just learning how to invest.

But what about the books on manifesting? Maybe you've diligently written your daily abundance affirmations, but still, nothing has changed. Shouldn't that have worked? Sigh. Are you doomed? Of course not!

Affirmations and manifesting exercises are great, but on their own they don't get to the core issues. They skim the surface without changing how we feel on a deep level. And what we *feel* is the key missing piece! But once we work on our core issues, affirmations can be very helpful. That's why

you'll find one at the end of each chapter to help anchor the deeper work you do as you work on the steps.

The Self-Worth Secret

In order to truly deal with our money issues, we need to go deep within and explore not just our feelings about money—but also our feelings about ourselves. That's because at heart, money issues are really issues of self-worth. In other words, *our self-worth determines our net worth.*

Until we truly feel worthy—deep inside—of the great life we desire, we won't feel worthy of money on the outside. When we *don't* feel worthy on the inside, we develop patterns that prevent us from having the money we want and need. For example, even if we get ourselves out of debt . . . we just build up more debt. Why would anybody do that? Well, they wouldn't do it on purpose. But these kinds of patterns are tenacious because they're created by unconscious feelings and negative beliefs that took hold in childhood.

In fact, our sense of self-worth is created when we're *very young.* As a result, some of us aren't even aware that we don't feel worthy inside. We carry unconscious beliefs about ourselves like "I'm not good enough," or "I'm not lovable," or "Other people are better than I am." These beliefs of unworthiness then drive our behaviors in all sorts of ways. Somebody with self-worth issues might want to go for a promotion but feel intimidated by the competition. This person might say, "Four other people are applying for that promotion? Oh . . . then I won't have a chance. I won't even put my name in the running."

The mash-up of money and self-worth issues starts early—and that's why we have to begin by uncovering those old worth issues from childhood. If we don't unwind the tangle of emotions and beliefs and fears that got encoded back then, we'll stay in a dysfunctional relationship with money . . . not to mention a dysfunctional relationship with ourselves. And it won't matter how many affirmations we write, or how much we learn about economics.

My client Darcy tried to learn about finance but couldn't get out from under her patterns borne of old self-worth issues. "Once I left my parents' house, I realized I needed to get my act together in order to support myself," she says, "but I had no concept of a budget or how to manage my money. So I was always short at the end of the month. I knew in my heart that I didn't want to live my life the way my parents did, paycheck to paycheck. I attended many workshops on budgeting and financial strategy. But every time, I would fall right back into the habit of spending money I didn't have. I'd work hard to pay off the debt, only to do it all over again. It was a crazy cycle."

What was the problem? Darcy needed to boost her self-worth before she could grow her net worth. No matter how much she learned about how to manage money, she couldn't make progress until she dealt with those deep feelings and unconscious beliefs—beliefs that were seriously limiting her ability to create the life she desired. Her story is a prime example of how our self-worth determines our net worth.

"Net Worth" and "Financial Freedom" Defined

Before I move on, I want to define a couple of phrases that are bandied about a lot when people talk about money. First, let's talk about "net worth." When I use this phrase, I don't just mean the amount of money you have or the assets you own. I'd never say that owning a lot of stuff or building up a huge stock portfolio is the key to happiness.

Yes, in this book, I'll talk a lot about money. But when I use "net worth," I really mean the degree of richness, juiciness, and fulfillment you have in all areas of your life, not just your bank account. Do you feel rich in your relationships? Do you have a wealth of activities you enjoy?

"High" net worth is a feeling of wholeness. In other words, I don't just want you to have more money, I want you to be free to create the life that makes you happy—whatever that means to you.

I like a quote by comedian Chris Rock on this subject: "Wealth is not about having a lot of money. It's about having a lot of options." If you have a high net worth, you have an abundance of opportunities.

What about "financial freedom"? Some people define it as having "plenty" of money (whatever that means to each individual) with investments that grow and with multiple revenue streams. For me, to be financially free means I'm no longer stuck in the dysfunctional patterns and belief system that kept me struggling to pay my bills or get out of debt. I'm not dependent upon somebody else for my money. And I don't spend my days feeling afraid I'm not going to have enough money—even when I'm doing just fine.

Financial freedom means being relaxed about money. Just stop for a second and imagine what that would feel like. Even people we call "rich" aren't necessarily relaxed about money. So instead of financial freedom, let's call it "financial ease."

What would financial ease look like? It would mean no longer being a slave to self-worth issues that cause problems with net worth. With financial ease, we'd have that wealth of opportunities. We'd no longer have the stress about money that takes so much energy away from the joys of life. We'd be able to do the things that supply that juiciness, that fulfill-ment, that *wholeness* I described.

And creating this full spectrum of high net worth starts with knowing that you're not just worthy of a life of financial ease. You're worthy of a life that makes you feel happy and fulfilled.

What's Your Worth Quotient?

The painful truth is this: If you want to see the state of your self-worth, all you have to do is look at your net worth. It's a direct reflection of how you feel about *you*. Do you currently have all the money you need? Do you feel capable of managing it well? Do you have a wealth of opportunities? If you couldn't honestly answer "yes" to those questions, you're probably dealing with some unconscious blocks around worth.

When we feel that we aren't enough, or that we aren't *good* enough, we also fear that we'll never *have* enough. That fear is a self-fulfilling prophecy, in which we unconsciously make sure we never, ever have all that we need. It's a pain-ful arithmetic going on in the shadows of our unconscious, which many of us never even recognize.

We have to get to the root of the problem, and that means replacing those feelings of unworthiness with a stron-ger sense of self-worth. We have to do the internal work to right this distorted view of ourselves in order to experience the freedom of wealth in our lives. Until we do that, we'll continue to subconsciously sabotage the very thing we're longing for. Ouch!

Take the person who wins the lottery—and promptly loses every penny because she never did the inner work to feel comfortable having that much money. Or take me! I once followed financial advice and invested money in a mutual fund, but I was so frightened that I watched the balance every day. Even though I knew how much the market could fluctuate, I got nervous and took all the money out before it could grow.

Once we've healed our internal wounds around worth, and we finally know we deserve good things, we open up to receiving more of what the universe has in store for us. We also change old behaviors that have gotten in our way. The more we believe in our worth, the less we're willing to continue destructive patterns. We say, "Wait! I deserve better than that!"

So if you have a problem with money, you need to look at what lies beneath. Suze Orman puts it this way: "You can't fix a financial problem with money. You can only fix a financial problem by fixing yourself. . . . You always have to go within to see why you are doing without."

The Tangle of Self-Worth and Net Worth

When we begin to let go of our unconscious limiting beliefs about our self-worth, money issues start to dissolve. It works in reverse, too! When we heal emotional wounds surrounding our finances, other areas of our life will begin to heal as well. It can almost feel miraculous.

My client Michele is a case in point. She married her husband when they were both young. Tragically, he died just a few years later, when Michele was only in her late 20s. He left her with plenty of money, but it made her uncomfortable. After all, he had earned it, not her. She didn't feel worthy of it. As a way of avoiding her discomfort, she hired a financial advisor to take care of the money for her. Then, she could just forget about it.

Over the next few years, rather than use the money her husband had left her, Michele charged everything . . . without the cash to pay off the debts each month. Technically, she was living in a state of abundance, but she couldn't take advantage of it. She was terrified to ask her financial advisor for her own money. Her father had scolded her in the past for some of her choices, so she found herself afraid her advisor would do the same. Maybe he would tell her she wasn't making wise choices. Maybe he would act like she didn't have a right to her own funds. Then, she'd feel put down and like a failure. Even though the money belonged to her, self-worth issues kept her paralyzed with fear.

When I started working with Michele, she told me that she had always wanted to move to Hawaii. But again, she didn't feel worthy of it. Gradually, we dug deep and examined her self-worth issues and how they were affecting her financial life. Through our work together—walking through the steps in this book—she was able to overcome her belief that she didn't have a right to do what she wanted. Even if her financial advisor didn't approve. Even if her father didn't like her choices.

And she did make it to Hawaii! How did she get there? With stronger feelings of self-worth, she was able to instruct her financial advisor to deposit money into her bank account each month. Of course, he agreed without hesitation. He didn't react as Michele had feared. She had hired him after all. It was his job to do as she asked.

But here's where the story gets really interesting. During our very first session, Michele confessed to me that she had been bulimic since the age of 19—and had been binging and purging every single day for the past 15 years. "I don't want to deal with that issue during our coaching, though," she'd said. Having already been to two eating disorder clinics, Michele was convinced nothing would work.

We never talked about her bulimia again and focused solely on her self-worth and money issues. That is, until January 2, 2015—six months after beginning our work together—when she called me to let me know that a miracle had happened. *She hadn't binged or purged for 24 hours.* It was her first day without bulimic behavior since she was 19 years old. As of the publication of this book, she hasn't binged and purged for months.

This doesn't necessarily mean that Michele's bulimia was a direct result of her fears about money. But it does indicate that her lack of self-worth and disempowerment were affecting not only her relationship to money but also her relationship to food. The work we did together around worthiness naturally had an impact on every aspect of her life. Her "net worth" increased in a number of ways beyond her bank balance.

Michele's story is not unusual. Hers is just a vivid example of how the entanglement of self-worth and net worth can create painful dramas in our lives.

Which is something I know all too well.

My Story

I'm not a CPA or a financial advisor. I'm no economics wizard. But I've *lived* what I'm going to teach you, and I've seen these steps in action. That doesn't mean I'm "Miss Perfect" when it comes to my self-worth or my relationship with money. This is a lifelong process, so I'm still working on both, believe me! But my self-worth and my patterns around money have made a 180-degree turn in the last few years. They're a far cry from where I started.

My money story isn't exactly typical, though. My family didn't struggle to make ends meet, so I was never in a situation of lack. My father is a dentist, and my mother stayed at home. I went to private school, and my parents paid for my college education. I didn't even have student loans like so many of my peers. I was blessed in many ways. At the same time, I really didn't have a clear understanding of, or relationship to, money while growing up.

Between undergraduate and graduate school, I lived in New York City for five years. I was completely self-supporting during that time. Many people admired my independence, given how much it costs to live in NYC and the fact that my parents probably would've helped me out if I'd asked. But while my independent streak is a virtue on one side, the flip side is that I have an underlying belief that no one will ever take care of my wants and needs. As illogical as it was, my limiting belief during those years was that I had no choice but to be independent.

In literally less than 24 hours after moving from New York City to Boulder, Colorado, I met the man who would become my husband. He was charming, sweet, and ruggedly handsome. And beneath his masculine bravado, the unspoken message from his psyche was, "I'm broken." My unspoken response? "Great! I'm Superwoman. I will fix you."

I drew a man toward me who was not only unable to take care of *my* wants and needs, but who was also unable to take care of his own. He was financially dependent upon *me*. When I met him, he had just moved back to town and didn't yet have a bank account. I'll never forget the day he walked through the door and gave me his first paycheck from his new job. "Can you deal with this?" he asked. Less than two weeks after we met, I was already managing his money. He was the kind of person who never looked at his

bank statements, while I'm the kind of person who balances her checkbook down to the penny.

As our relationship progressed, he was in and out of jobs and not terribly interested in working. Meanwhile, I was busy building my career as an event producer, traveling and working for different organizations around the country. By the time I landed my job as event director at Hay House in my mid-30s, my career was in full swing. I was doing work I loved and making great money. My husband, on the other hand, was still lost, floundering, and constantly trying different things. While I'm not judging him for this—in fact, I enabled him—it was hardly a healthy situation for either of us.

I ended up buying him almost anything he wanted . . . from motorcycles to condos. I bought him a brand-new truck, paid in cash, just three months before I left the marriage. Meanwhile, I rarely spent money on myself. I made money and promptly spent it on him because I was trying to make him happy. I had grown up with everything I wanted, and he had grown up with nothing. I wanted desperately to heal his wounds. "I don't need anything. I don't want anything. Whatever you want," I would say. Of course, I was also trying to buy his love because of my own issues with self-worth.

After losing a lot financially in the divorce agreement, I was so frightened of spending that I became a bit of a miser. I managed to amass what I consider to be a large sum, but I kept it all where I could see it, in a low interest–bearing savings account. When I finally consulted with a financial advisor, she said, "You keeping all that money in a savings account is like planting frozen vegetables and expecting them to grow." Still, I had always felt that investing in the stock market was like gambling. It was too much risk for me. What if I lost it all? My belief was that no one would ever be there to catch me.

Rather than force me out of my comfort zone too soon, my very wise financial advisor played on my desire to save. "Over the course of the next several years, you'll pay an exorbitant sum in interest on your mortgage. Why don't you use some of the money in your account to pay it off?" What? Such a thing had never even dawned on me.

But after being shown the numbers, I couldn't deny that it was a smart choice that would free me financially and emotionally. So in November of 2014, I walked a very large cashier's check two blocks from Wells Fargo to Chase, and I paid off my mortgage. It was surreal! A part of me freaked out because I felt like I was "spending" so much money.

When I handed the check to the representative at the bank, he said, "You're living the American dream!" I had no credit card debt, and I now owned my home outright.

My advisor then helped me put the rest of my funds in the highest-earning savings account available and also start an IRA.

I would never have been able to do any of that if I hadn't spent the previous few years diving deeply into my feelings of unworthiness and turning them around. It was only through increasing my self-worth that I finally decided I even deserved to consult a financial advisor in the first place!

So even though my story about money might differ from yours, I really have been in the trenches. And I've become certified in two separate life-coaching programs that forced me to explore my deepest wounds from childhood. I'm not going to tell you it was always fun, but it has changed my life for the better in more ways than I can count—both in terms of my self-worth and my net worth. Money, fulfillment, juiciness, opportunities, and happiness—they've all increased for me as a result of doing the work I'm going to outline for you on these pages. I was able to take responsibility for my

choices, quit my job, launch my dream career, and achieve financial ease. If you're willing to work these steps, I think you can achieve dramatic results, too.

Walk This Path with Me

In the pages that follow, I'll give you what most personal finance books lack—a process for working through your underlying emotional and psychological roadblocks to greater self-worth and net worth. I'll share more of my own story, and you'll read about many of my clients who have made big shifts in their lives. It isn't magic. It isn't luck. It isn't manifesting. You'll do the same exercises as my clients to discover what's standing in your way.

These are some of the questions you'll explore as you move through the steps: What are your secrets around money? What do you not want to admit to yourself? Why do you feel you don't deserve to be financially free? How much has your unwillingness to face money issues cost you—literally and figuratively? Are you spending money to numb yourself out? To make yourself feel better? To take care of others? Are you more comfortable staying in the dark about your finances because that's the way it's always been? What are you afraid to see?

Here's the plan:

Step One: Take Off the Blinders. In this step, you'll get real about the money issues you face every day. What do you ignore? Where do you put your head in the sand?

Step Two: Admit Who Holds the Purse Strings. Next, you'll think about who—or what—actually holds the purse strings in your life.

Step Three: Take Inventory of Your Beliefs. This step really gets to the heart of the matter. You'll discover your limiting beliefs about money and your own self-worth.

Step Four: Tally the Cost of Your Excuses. What excuses do you use to avoid creating the life you really want? Once you know, it will be harder to let them hold you back.

Step Five: Uncover Your Underlying Commitments. This step will show you how you're always getting exactly what you're committed to. It's just that your commitments may not be what you think!

Step Six: Become Willing to Be Worthy. Now that you have a good idea of the deeper issues that have been in your way, you can boost your self-worth and let yourself have more of the "good stuff."

Step Seven: Take Back Your Financial Power. In this step, you'll empower yourself to take responsibility for your financial life and make sure you're the one in the driver's seat.

Step Eight: Make One Powerful Financial Decision. All you have to do to start is make one change. Alter the course of just one of your patterns around money, and you're on your way.

Step Nine: Uncover Your Desires—Financial and Otherwise. It's great to feel more worthy, but what do you truly want? This step will help you not only get in touch with your desires but help you expand what you believe is possible for you, financially and in other areas of your life, too.

Step Ten: Get Ready to Do the Impossible. When you dismantle long-held beliefs and patterns about your worth, amazing things begin to happen—even what you once thought was impossible.

Steps One through Five are all about discovering what's in your way. In Steps Six through Ten, we'll get to the brass tacks of making positive changes inside and outside—from increasing your feelings of worthiness to putting your new positive beliefs into action. From there, you can begin to create the life you've always wanted.

Sounds exhilarating, yes? Well, it is! Take it from me and scores of my coaching clients.

If you feel more anxiety than exhilaration, don't worry. I know that the thought of digging into your past can bring up some fears. But you won't be thrown into the deep end! If you start to feel afraid, just breathe. We'll do this together. I promise you can do it! As I walk with you through the process, each step will prepare you for the next. And you'll move through it at your own speed.

Do You Need to Write Down the Exercises?

Every chapter will include exercises. It's important that you write down your answers to each of these because frequently, I will ask you to refer to your answers. You can record them in a paper journal, on your computer, or on another device. Just make sure that you keep them as you read!

I also encourage you to reflect on what you discover about yourself as you go through this process, and write down any thoughts and feelings that come up. Give yourself the time that you deserve. It's an opportunity for you to dive deeper into the power of writing and journaling, and you'll be able to see the evidence of your progress because you'll have a written record of it!

You'll find within you the courage and willingness to allow the unseen to be seen, the unknown to be known, and the uncomfortable to become comfortable. Doors will open. Light bulbs will go off. You may even experience some fireworks. For sure, you'll see yourself—and your life—with new eyes. You'll become open to the kind of financial ease and independence you've always wanted. And, of course, a new relationship with yourself will be the best part—a free bonus gift that will pay dividends in every area of your life. You're worth it, so let's do it!

TAKE OFF
THE BLINDERS

Anne had a history of building up credit card debt, paying it off, and building it up again—a common hamster wheel for many people. "I never read a credit card statement or considered the amount of interest I'd been paying," she says. "Here's the cost of my avoidance: My mortgage is at an 8 percent interest rate, and because my credit score is so low, I can't refinance at the average 2 percent available today. But that's nothing compared with the shame I've felt and the impact my spending has had on my family. My habits are now showing up in my 21-year-old daughter. I see her pull out a credit card to pay for something without the slightest thought of the consequences."

Anne's self-worth has taken a hit as a result of all this. But the truth is that it's low self-worth that caused her to put on the blinders in the first place.

Whether we make our own money or rely on someone else, many of us would rather pretend our financial matters don't exist. Or we hope they'll just take care of themselves somehow. My ex-husband was like that. He always said, "I bank by prayer. I go to the ATM and pray that money will come out."

Why do we put prefer not to look at reality? Well, many of us feel like we'd actually be blinded if we looked directly at our financial problems. Just the thought sends us to bed, with armloads of popcorn and chocolate, ready to binge-watch our favorite trashy TV show. Trust me—I get it. I've been there. (An episode or two of *Nashville*, anyone?)

So to avoid being blinded, we put on metaphorical blinders. We continue to live our lives on automatic, perpetuating the same patterns day in and day out. After all, confronting our money issues would force us to confront our feelings of self-worth . . . or lack thereof. And uncovering those feelings can feel a little like an archaeological dig. It's dusty and scary down there, where our unconscious beliefs have been hiding all this time. So we stay in the same old situations because we're comforted by the familiar—even if the familiar is terrible. "Better the devil you know than the devil you don't," and all that. In order to avoid looking at our deepest wounds, we unconsciously create situations in which money is a problem for us.

In the Introduction, I said that you can easily see the state of your self-worth by looking at your net worth. So the first step in this process—before you do anything else—is to *take off the blinders and look at what you've been hiding from regarding your finances.*

Now, don't worry. This isn't going to be a big confrontation. No need to grab the ice cream and the remote. The exercises in this first chapter are gentle and will ease you into the process. Throughout the steps of the book, you'll gradually unpack more and more of the deep-seated self-worth issues that caused you to turn a blind eye in the first place. Then, the natural next step will be to get your financial world in order. You can pick up one of those other books to help you learn all about investing and such. (I recommend Suze

Orman—see the Resources section.) And you'll want to do it because as a result of this process, you'll know you're worth it!

First, though, let's try an exercise that allows you to put all your cards on the table.

EXERCISE #1: COMPLAIN AWAY

Those of us into self-growth and spirituality are often told to stop complaining and focus on the positive. "Stop talking about what's wrong—or you'll just get more of it!" they tell us. Well, here's your chance to throw that instruction out the window. (Admit it—doesn't that sound kind of fun?)

1. Write down all of your complaints about money. What drives you crazy? What do you hate?

2. What are the problems you face every day regarding money?

3. Who or what stands in the way of your financial ease? Lay all your cards on the table—no holds barred.

4. What do you not want to think about regarding your money? What makes you want to turn a blind eye or run screaming from the room?

5. Once you've emptied it all out on paper (or on-screen), take a deep breath. There it all is. This is your "money myth"—what you might have told yourself is your lot in life. Only it isn't your fate, and you're going to start changing it right now. Don't toss out this money myth, though, because we'll be working with it again in a later chapter!

6. For now, however, write these words at the bottom of the page: "My new life of high self-worth, high net worth, and financial ease begins now." There—you've set your intention. Now, let's keep going.

Come Out of Hiding

Setting an intention is important. It energizes us in the direction of what we truly desire. But it doesn't mean we get to keep our head in the sand. If we want to make changes in our financial situation, we have to stop hiding from it.

Eileen, for example, told herself that the world of finance was "boring." Throughout her life, she'd either struggled with money or was completely dependent on someone else to take care of her needs. In her marriage, her husband was the breadwinner, while she stayed home to care for the kids. There's certainly nothing wrong with that, but when the children grew up and moved out, Eileen didn't know what to do with herself. Then, unexpectedly, her husband lost some of his income—leaving Eileen feeling lost.

"I've been so disconnected from our finances all this time, and now our financial situation is going downhill. I feel helpless, almost childlike. It's like I'm now having to grow up and relearn all that I've taken for granted," she says. "As a result, I've been feeling totally unworthy. If I ever had to go it alone, I honestly don't know if I could do it. I always thought I avoided learning about finances because they didn't interest me," she admits, "but now, I realize the 'boredom' was resistance because I was afraid."

That's the cost of hiding from our money matters. It may feel easier to avoid them now, but that avoidance usually makes things more difficult in the future. And that's hardly the future you've set your intention toward!

You've already written down the financial problems you've been experiencing. Now, let's delve deeper into where you might be hiding. Do you "bank by prayer" like my ex-husband used to do? Are you veering toward an uncertain financial future? Whatever your habits, confronting where you've turned a blind eye will help you begin to set your course for a brighter, more certain future.

EXERCISE #2: TAKE STOCK OF YOUR FINANCIAL HABITS AND PATTERNS

This is a list of common destructive money habits and patterns. It will help you begin to see where you've put on the blinders and gone into hiding. Open your journal or your computer/tablet. Now, read over the statements below, and copy down any that feel true for you. When you finish, you'll have a list of your particular money patterns. For now, just hold on to the list. You don't have to do anything specific about it . . . yet.

1. I often run out of money before my bills are paid.

2. I maintain credit card debt.

3. I don't look at or reconcile my bank statements.

4. I don't look at my credit card statements.

5. I don't know how much interest I'm being charged.

6. I don't have a savings account.

7. I don't have a retirement account.

8. I have a retirement account, but I don't contribute to it regularly.

9. I don't know how much money I spend regularly.

10. I haven't created a budget, or I've created one and don't stick to it.

11. I often pay late fees.

12. I put off paying my bills.

13. I maintain an overdraft at my bank.

14. I rarely, if ever, look at my credit report.

15. I don't know my credit score.

16. I owe back taxes.

17. I don't have any money of my own.

18. I haven't been in the workforce for a long time.

19. I don't have any marketable skills.

20. I don't know anything about our finances.

21. My spouse takes care of all of our money matters.

22. I don't know how much I'm worth financially.

23. I don't have a will or other estate documents.

24. If anything happened to my spouse, I don't know if I'd be okay financially.

25. I shop compulsively.

26. I'm afraid if I spend any money, I'll end up destitute.

27. No matter how hard I try, I never seem to have enough money.

28. Since I don't earn the money myself, I feel guilty when I spend it.

29. I tend to give away my products or services.

30. I don't charge as much as I should for my products or services.

31. I'm afraid to ask for a raise or a promotion.

32. I work in a job I hate.

33. I would like to have a different career.

34. I don't know what I really want to do for a living.

35. I have always relied on others to take care of me financially.

36. I don't know how to take care of myself financially.

37. Money seems to burn a hole in my pocket.

38. I spend money on other people but rarely on myself.

39. I like to treat myself with things I can't really afford.

Add your own statements:

1. _____

2. _____

3. _____

4. _____

5. _____

If you find that you've copied down more of these than you hoped, don't use it as an excuse to beat up on yourself. Remember that you're taking action by working this process, so you're already on your way to changing your financial habits and patterns. It's only a matter of time!

The Guilt Game

There are lots of reasons why we avoid the truth about our finances. In the remainder of the chapter, we'll talk about some of the most common ones. First up—guilt. It's a biggie, especially for women!

Yes, men carry a lot of guilt about money, too, but we women seem to have it in spades. Studies show that women are less likely to negotiate their salary or ask for a raise. If we do and are told there's no money in the budget, we're more likely to give in, feeling guilty for asking in the first place. Men, on the other hand, are far more apt to stand their ground and keep pushing until they get what they want.

Now, I won't go into all the feminist issues about how women have been taught these behaviors on a cultural level. There are already plenty of books on that subject, too! Whatever the reason, we women have self-worth issues that tend to come out in particular ways around money—and we often put our heads in the sand as a result.

For example, women are also more prone to putting loved ones first, and to feeling guilty if we spend money on ourselves. Nobody likes guilty feelings, so we do whatever's necessary to avoid it—even if it means turning a blind eye to how much we reject our own wants and needs.

I have a friend whose mother wanted another dog very much but decided it was too expensive. At the same time, she had no problem spending money on whatever her grandchildren wanted. She denied herself because she felt she was less worthy than the people she loved. And she had a belief that it was more righteous to give to others.

While it's wonderful to love others and give to them, giving and receiving must be kept in balance if we want to maintain a healthy relationship with ourselves and our finances. With healthier self-worth, we take care of ourselves just as well as we take care of everybody else. No guilt required. And, therefore, blinders off.

Many of us also believe that if we have more, others will have less. We feel guilty for having abundance. But spiritual teachers throughout the ages, and even physicists like Einstein, have taught that everything is energy—even money. So the energy of money is always available, since energy is never lost— it just changes form. Financial abundance is infinite.

Fear of Our Own Greatness

There's another reason we tend to avoid the truth, and it's even harder to recognize. What would happen if our hard-luck stories related to money turned out *not* to be true? What if we *deserved* and *could have* an infinite financial future? If that were true, it would invalidate a whole bunch of ideas we have about ourselves. Like, for example, the idea that we aren't worthy! We'd have to expand our current comfort level to having more. We'd have to stop playing small.

I know this Marianne Williamson quote has been used a lot, but I can't resist it because it's so wonderful and perfect for this point:

Our deepest fear is not that we are inadequate. Our deepest fear is that we are powerful beyond measure. It is our light, not our darkness that most frightens us. We ask ourselves, Who am I to be brilliant, gorgeous, talented, fabulous? Actually, who are you not to be? You are a child of God. Your playing small does not serve the world. There's nothing enlightened about shrinking so that other people won't feel insecure around you. We are all meant to shine, as children do. We were born to make manifest the glory of God that is within us. It's not just in some of us; it's in everyone. And as we let our own light shine, we unconsciously give other people permission to do the same. As we're liberated from our own fear, our presence automatically liberates others.

Are you playing small in your life to keep your family or friends comfortable? Are you playing small in order to pay allegiance to outworn, false beliefs?

My client Sheila makes beautiful "intention" bracelets. But for some reason, she had a belief that she should just give them away—even when people were ready and willing to pay her for her work.

"I was at a convention recently, and there was a woman there who wanted some of my bracelets," Sheila explains. "She bought 25 bracelets, and I charged her a price that felt great to me. I was so excited. But then she told a friend of mine that she wanted to buy 100 more. My first reaction was 'Oh, I can't charge her as much if she's buying so many. I would feel really bad. It would be a lot of money.' My friend said, 'She knows how much they are, and she asked for them. So don't even give it a thought.'"

But it was still difficult for Sheila to think about taking the money. Part of her wanted to tell the woman to just take the bracelets for free. "Back when I owned a store, somebody new would come in and I would give them merchandise for free or only charge them half price," Sheila says. "I was afraid this woman would see the invoice for the bracelets and say, 'Oh, I didn't realize they were that much. I don't want them.' I went to a class one day and brought all my bracelets with me. I had them out, and people loved them. But I gave them all away—I wouldn't take any money for them."

Sheila's bracelets are pieces of her—pieces she was giving away. Her self-worth issues made her blind to the value she has to offer the world.

As a result of our coaching work, Sheila printed out an invoice for the 100 bracelets ahead of time and handed it to the woman who ordered them. Even though Sheila was shaking in her shoes, the woman gladly paid the invoice without questioning it. This was a big step for Sheila to begin to see that her work is valued by others. Now she has a website with her complete line of bracelets for sale, and she feels great about charging for them!

Accepting our greatness means no longer playing small. It often starts with baby steps. But eventually it means making major changes—in our lives, jobs, relationships, and dreams. If I had believed in my own self-worth, I would never have been willing to make the financial moves I made in the past. If I'd known my value, I couldn't have spent so many years ignoring the whispering—and sometimes screaming—voice that told me to leave my marriage. For a long time, that truth was just too scary and painful for me to face. Talk about keeping my head in the sand! But how many years did I waste, postponing what has proven to be a much better life—simply because I went into hiding and didn't see that I was worthy of something better?

When we change and grow into new versions of ourselves, we have to tolerate a lot of uncertainty. That's what my book *Jump . . . And Your Life Will Appear* is all about. Rather than face uncertainty, most of us stay stuck for years in family patterns, adopting our parents' money habits, and making sure we keep those blinders tightly over our eyes! Many of us believe that sticking with the status quo will win us love and belonging. In order to avoid uncertainty and to feel as though we belong, we hold to long-held cultural beliefs, following the prescribed paths we've been told will make us happy. These paths take the pressure off of us. We don't have to forge new pathways. We can stay "safe" in the roles of daughter, son, wife, husband, mother, or father. We don't have to have difficult conversations where we break the norms and expectations our family and loved ones have of us.

But how safe are these roles *really*? How safe is it to play so small that we squeeze ourselves into boxes and live false lives? How safe is it to play so small that we give ourselves away, reinforcing the belief that we have no real worth?

These beliefs that we hold about money—and our own worthiness—keep us in situations that aren't truly satisfying. They trap us in the fear of the unknown, where we're willing to short ourselves to avoid stepping outside of our comfort zone. The tragedy is that so many of us are willing to stay small to such a degree that we squander the beautiful lives we've been given.

I'm here to convince you that it's time to do things differently.

The good news is that we all have infinite potential. As Thomas Edison is quoted as saying, "If we did all the things we are capable of doing, we would literally astound ourselves." Wow!

An infinite attitude toward money and our own self-worth starts with taking off the blinders and seeing where we've kept ourselves in the dark.

Are You Stuffing Your Feelings in Your Jimmy Choos (or Your Kate Spade Bag)?

When an unpleasant feeling rises to the surface, do you run to the mall or plug in your credit card number at your favorite website? Spending addictions are common with both men and women, but especially with women. Talk about turning a blind eye to reality and running on autopilot!

Sure, it's exhilarating to have that new handbag on your arm, or this season's hottest new boots on your feet. But shopping can be just another way of avoiding what we really feel. And for many of us, it means debt.

My client Giselle tells a story about her love affair with her credit cards. "My first credit card was a Sears card. I really had nothing back then. I never felt like my mother loved me. I never felt like anybody loved me. But Sears gave me a credit card. It had a $400 limit. There wasn't a big selection at Sears, but I loved that card. There were a few cute things I could buy, so I maxed it out right away. We were fast friends."

Today, Giselle has seven credit cards. "They're like a mistress would be," she says. "They're my secret. They fill my needs, make me pretty, and do whatever I say. I know it's false, but it feels real. I'm getting adored by the card and lavished with gifts as if it were a boyfriend. If I feel lonely or empty, I can go out and use the card for a beautiful dinner or beautiful clothes and feel, again, like I'm being taken care of. And I'm not lonely anymore. Even if I go out to eat by myself and use the credit card, it's like I'm not by myself. It's like I'm with a very, very close lover and friend who knows exactly what I want."

Giselle's favorite card is her United MileagePlus card. "I get a free checked bag at the airport. I know it seems silly, but it really feels like a man taking care of me or a mother taking care of me. The limit is up to $24,000 right now with 20 percent interest. It makes me feel rich and really taken care of. Spending, for me, is like beauty, like an event. It's like love. I feel important. If I'm on vacation, and I want to go to the spa or stay at a nice hotel, the card takes care of that for me. Even when I pay the bill, I don't connect to the fact that I'm really the one taking care of me."

Giselle points out that her credit cards never judge her or say no to her. "They're like my harem. If I want to get something and one card is maxed out, the other card steps in for me. Spending is better than sex because it isn't about what I look like. Even if I'm feeling fat, there's no judgment from my card. I once spent $10,000 on a Chanel suit. I remember that feeling of putting it in my car—it was like a drug deal. I've never done heroin, but I'll bet it feels like that."

Giselle knows that she can't keep up this "love affair." It feels safe, but it's a poor substitute for the real kind of love she deserves with a human being. Her story illustrates how much of an addiction spending can become and how much we learn to rely on it—just like addicts rely on alcohol or drugs or food.

If you're like Giselle—drowning your sorrows in a Chanel suit or a spa day you can't afford—it's time for a change. The love you're looking for can't be found in a little plastic card, no matter how many handbags it will buy you.

Facing Your Feelings about Finances

When we overspend like Giselle, or hoard money like I did, or avoid looking at our finances altogether, what we're *really* avoiding are our feelings. And remember, I said this book is all about how we *feel* about money.

There are certain emotions we like to feel—like happiness, gratitude, love, and excitement. Other feelings? Not so much. Whatever it is we're not looking at, you can bet it's associated with those "let's just pretend we don't feel that" emotions. As you work through the process in this book, feelings *will* come up. Get ready for them! We've already talked about guilt. Other feelings might include, but are certainly not limited to: sadness, hurt, anger, rage, resentment, and shame.

These are the feelings we spend most of our lives avoiding, so it's no surprise that we don't volunteer to spend time in their company. Yet the effort to push them away is what keeps us stuck.

Here's what I've learned from experience: These emotions may be unpleasant, but *they won't kill you!* I promise. It starts with taking a different perspective: You *have* feelings. You *are not* your feelings. They're visitors that stay for a short time and pass through. Allowing them to have their little visit in your consciousness will make room for new, more pleasant feelings to follow. In other words, feeling the not-so-fun stuff will free you up so you're available when the good stuff comes calling.

Part of the not-so-fun stuff is looking at how our unwillingness to face reality is directly related to how worthy we feel. For the first half of the book, we're spending a lot of time removing the blinders and getting to what's below the surface. So before we dig deeper, let's take a moment to reset the clock and start fresh.

EXERCISE #3: THE POWER OF COMPASSION AND FORGIVENESS

We just talked about some of the feelings that can come up when you're working on financial and self-worth issues. I suspect you've had some uncomfortable feelings come up as a result of taking a look at how you've turned a blind eye to money matters. You might be feeling like the state of your net worth is reflecting a sad state of self-worth. So before we move on, let's take a moment to ease some of the discomfort and regain some equilibrium.

1. Take a deep breath, and exhale out any shame or guilt or sadness you feel about the state of your net worth and self-worth. Take several more breaths, and continue to exhale out any dark feelings that have come up. Affirm that you won't use this assessment as an excuse to beat yourself up. After all, you don't want to create even lower self-worth by chastising yourself over low self-worth—talk about a double whammy!

2. Take another deep breath. This time, breathe in the energy of forgiveness. Begin to forgive yourself for the moments in the past that you've hidden from your money matters. While you'll do a lot in this process to look at the past and how it's affecting you now, affirm that you're wiping the slate clean with no blame or shame. You're starting from now.

3. Remind yourself that you're reading this book now, so you're on your way to a new beginning. It's the start of boosting your self-worth and growing your net worth. Reiterate the intention you set in Exercise #1: "My new

life of high self-worth, high net worth, and financial ease begins now."

Affirm Your Worth

"I see my current financial situation honestly and know that I'm worthy of creating financial ease."

ADMIT WHO HOLDS THE PURSE STRINGS

Faye's life seemed great . . . then her husband came to her with a shocker. He revealed that he had a gambling addiction and had lost all of their money. "We were $40,000 in debt, and both his job and our house were suddenly in jeopardy," she says. Faye, Eileen in the last chapter, and many other women, willingly hand over control of their finances to someone else. It might be their husband, a parent, a financial advisor or CPA, or even their children. But doing so can bring up a host of issues, both internal and external.

Take Beth. She stayed in what she calls a "twenty-five-year, lonely, empty marriage with a porn addict" because she was terrified she would be destitute without her husband. "I built myself that prison," she says, "and I stayed for financial security." More than a decade ago, she was finally able to boost her self-worth enough to leave the marriage. But ever since, she's been living off the money from her divorce settlement . . . and that money is now running out. To keep things going, she's started dipping into her retirement fund. Now, here she is, in her early 60s, faced with the necessity of making a living for herself for the first time in her life. It's taking another boost of her self-worth to get out there and take care of her finances.

Both Faye and Beth have learned the hard way what can happen when we let someone else hold the purse strings in our lives. And relinquishing our purse strings is just another way that we hide from our money matters.

We all know the adage: "He who controls the purse strings rules the world." So in a certain way, our purse strings are our "life strings." In other words, if you want to know who's in charge of your life, ask yourself who's in charge of your money.

That's why Step Two is *admit who holds the purse strings in your life.* How much responsibility do you have with regard to your money? Who is the CFO of your personal world?

What's It Like to Hold the Purse Strings?

When we hold the purse strings in our lives, we're empowered to make the financial decisions we want to make. Certainly, if we're in partnership and have joint finances, we'll consult with our partner before making a big purchase. But that's very different from having to ask *permission.* If our self-worth is strong, we don't feel comfortable having to ask for someone else's consent to spend money.

In fact, with a keen sense of worthiness, we won't allow anyone else to completely control our money. We just won't stand for it. That doesn't mean we become control freaks. It doesn't mean we don't trust our partner. It just means that we refuse to give all of our power away to anyone else, no matter who it is.

When we relinquish our financial volition, on the other hand, we give ourselves some dangerous permissions. First, we don't have to make difficult decisions—or *any* decisions around money. Second, we don't have to make the mistakes, because the responsibility is on someone else. Finally, we don't have to educate ourselves about financial issues. What all of this means is that, if things go wrong, we can point the finger at the person in control. We don't have to confront our feelings of not deserving. It also means we don't have to grow up. Let's face it: Being a grown-up is scary.

But we give up a lot in exchange for handing over the purse strings. We put ourselves in the position of playing the role of victim, at the mercy of someone else's decision-making.

Everything in the book from now on will help you get better hold of your purse strings because you'll work on the obstacles to greater self-worth. All of that will culminate in Step Seven, Take Back Your Financial Power, and beyond to Step Ten. For now, we're only on a mission of discovery. You aren't going to make any changes yet regarding your purse strings. You'll need to move through some more of the steps before it's time to safely make direct changes. If you try to make shifts too fast, you could easily fall back into old habits. So in this chapter, be content with uncovering where you've handed over control. That alone is an important part of the process!

What If You Aren't the Breadwinner?

Since this is such a common issue with my female clients, here's a place where I'll break my rule and give you some actual financial advice.

Like Faye at the beginning of the chapter, often the husband is the sole source of money in the family. The female partner—or sometimes the male partner, as in my own marriage—has no money of their own. In my family, my mother was in that situation, so my parents solved it this way: Even though Mom didn't work outside the home, my father gave her a regular monthly check. She would use it to buy groceries, keep the house, and pay for things for us kids. She could then spend or save whatever was left for herself.

I encourage my clients who aren't making money of their own to have an agreement with their spouse that compensates them for the work they do at home. We have a false belief in our society that housework and raising children are tasks not worthy of monetary compensation. But if you hire a maid to clean your house or a nanny to care for your children, you have no qualms about paying them, do you? Why should a wife or mother be any different? If there are funds available, wives and mothers are entitled to some of that money for themselves in compensation for all that they do.

When my niece was very young, she told a friend of hers that her mother got her out of bed in the morning, made her breakfast, fixed her lunch, took her to school, picked her up, and took her to classes and practices all over town. What did Daddy do? He just went to one place all day long. How's that for perspective?

If you're in this situation, besides negotiating an agreement to receive monetary compensation for your work at home, I encourage you to develop marketable skills. While you may never use them, having skills that could help you get a job if you ever wanted one will heighten your sense of self-worth and help you feel more secure. You won't carry around the worry that you'll be left in the lurch if, God forbid, you're forced to work outside the home at some point in the future. Even if you only have time to develop the skills very gradually, it's worth it to start now.

Let's come out of hiding right away. Take an inventory of the skills you could offer someone tomorrow. What could you do if you needed or wanted a job or if you wanted to get a better or different position? If you need help, ask a trusted friend to brainstorm about your skills with you. We tend to downplay our own talents and skills, thinking they hold little value. Try to write down ten or more. I guarantee that you have more to offer than you think!

Money, the Manipulator

Whenever you're talking about money, you're talking about control. Money makes the world go round, as they say. There's a power that comes with being able to exchange currency for the things we want and need in life. This is, in part, why money issues can be so dicey. Money control can show up in all sorts of paradoxical and manipulative ways. A parent might give an adult child money as a way of obligating the child to behave in ways the parent prefers. Even if the money appears to be freely given, there's often a price tag for taking a loan from a friend or loved one. The same can happen in a couple where one partner is the breadwinner. He or she may exert control by complaining and criticizing the nonworking partner's spending practices, since they're not the one actually earning the bread.

Then there's Lizzie. The purse strings in her situation weren't really held by her husband, but more by his parents. "My husband had a huge pattern of losing jobs, and we would dig ourselves into this horrible financial hole. Each time, his parents would pay us out of it," she explains. Then, the same thing would happen again.

Eventually, she told her husband that she'd leave if the pattern continued. "I'll do whatever it takes for us to be independent," she told him. "But you have to get on board with me. You have to admit to this pattern and the fact that it's not sustainable." Unfortunately, her husband refused to face the truth and decided to remain dependent on his parents. So Lizzie felt she had to leave the marriage.

Getting divorced has put her in a tenuous position financially, but at least she's holding the purse strings now. She's taken back control of her finances, and can continue to improve her circumstances. She recently got her house out of foreclosure and paid off all her debt. Even though she's still living paycheck to paycheck for now, she says, "I feel so much freer, so different. I'm relieved and so much happier. And I feel like a better mother and a better person just because I admitted our financial situation was a disaster and took responsibility for changing things."

During our coaching, Lizzie realized that she'd made herself out to be the victim, and her husband the perpetrator. She knew that she, too, was responsible for the situation they were in—doing her part by relinquishing her power. In leaving the marriage, she made her first financial decision in years: she took back control and took herself out of the victim role.

Too many of us are like marionettes, with someone else controlling the (purse) strings. If we don't believe we're capable of handling the finances, it's often a sign that we don't feel confident in our capacity to handle our *lives*. So we give our power away to others in the form of money control—and often the money ends up controlling *us*. So ask yourself: How much power and control do you feel in your life? Would your situation change dramatically if you were the one holding the purse strings? And most importantly, are you controlling your money, or is your money controlling you?

EXERCISE #4: WHO CONTROLS THE PURSE STRINGS IN YOUR LIFE?

This step is about identifying who might be in control of your financial world. Ask yourself the following questions to begin to discover if someone has a hold on your purse strings. Make note of any feelings, beliefs, or insights that pop up as you answer the questions. (If you don't have to answer to anyone else in regard to money matters, you can skip this exercise. The next exercise will apply to you!)

1. Do you need to consult someone else for approval or permission before making a big purchase? If so, who?

2. Does that same person consult you if he or she is making a big purchase?

3. Who controls your bank account?

4. Who pays the household bills?

5. Does anyone other than you have a direct stake in your finances?

6. Does anyone try to control or manipulate you with money? If so, how do they do it?

7. How does it feel to have someone else control your finances? Does it help you feel safe? Or do you feel controlled and out of control?

8. How would it feel to have 100 percent control over your money? Would you feel elated? Lost? Scared? All of the above?

What's Holding the Purse Strings Is Never Actually a Person

Did the heading of this section surprise you? Yep, even if we've given control over our finances to another human being, the real culprit—what's *really* holding the purse strings—is lack of self-worth. Not to mention the fears and limitations that come with it. That's the reason we're allowing someone else to have control over our money, right?

In my case, it looked like I held the purse strings in my marriage. After all, I was the one with the money. But looking back, I see that I didn't really have control over my finances. My decisions were driven in large part by my desire to control my husband's rage and disapproval. I used money to placate him and to gain his love. I may have technically earned the money, but how I spent it was really controlled by him. In truth, I had given him all of my power.

Sometimes there's plenty of money available, but we still don't feel worthy of holding our own purse strings. Take Blair. Her husband is the breadwinner in the family, but he tells her to spend their money as she likes. Still, Blair feels tremendous guilt about buying anything that's not absolutely essential, because she hasn't earned the money herself. Recently, she treated herself to a personal trainer, but she gets a pit in her stomach every time she has to pay him. Meanwhile, she has no problem paying for her kids to participate in every extra-curricular activity under the sun!

What about those of us who don't have to ask permission of anyone to spend money, but we're still in debt? The purse strings aren't held by another person, but we're hardly driving our own carriage. We're really in the backseat (with blinders on, by the way) while we let our fears and emotions and beliefs and self-worth issues take the reins.

There are all sorts of ways that we can inadvertently relinquish our purse strings. Which brings us to Maggie, who has never had to worry about money. Sounds great, right? But here's the problem: "Money has never been a motivating factor for me, because I've been taken care of," she says. "Looking back, I realize how much this has held me back from living my dreams. I tend to be fearful of moving forward, and the fact that I wasn't pushed made it easier to stay put. I never paid much attention to finances, and now, I want to be more independent in this area. I feel childlike, having been taken care of all these years. So I guess the obstacle was having someone take care of me and the need to feel safe and small. Now, even though I don't have to work, I want to feel the empowerment of holding my own purse strings."

Maggie's lack of financial need allowed her self-worth issues to remain unconscious. She was able to hide from her fears of testing her talents and stay "safe and small." As a result, she never took control of her purse strings.

If we're really holding the strings, we aren't a slave to our fears. We don't hide from anything in regard to money. You already know the key to taking control of your purse strings in a healthy way. You guessed it—stronger self-worth! It'll always come back to that.

Control Through Overspending

Like Giselle in the last chapter, some of us might try to create a sense of control through overspending. But as long as we're spending to avoid feelings, we're still letting our money control *us*.

Having money can be confronting to those of us who have a deep, unconscious identity that says, "I'm not worthy." In that case, it's uncomfortable to have money in the bank, so the funds burn a hole in our pocket. It's like the musician who suddenly becomes a big success, only to spend the money quickly and end up bankrupt. It isn't that this person is necessarily irresponsible. But do they feel inherently worthy of the big bank balance? Probably not. They feel safer if they run it down to a level that's more congruent with their beliefs about themselves.

If this is your pattern, you may have noticed that there's an inner fight going on between the part of you that wants to feel you deserve . . . and the part of you that believes you don't. That conflict can cause enough inner turmoil to send you off on yet another spending binge.

Often, we believe something outside of us is going to make us worthy. Maybe it's the "right" clothes, the "right" car or the "right" house. Sure, these things may help us feel abundant. But it can be easy to get caught in the trap of faking it until we make it . . . all the way to a credit card balance that makes our eyeballs pop out. We simply have to do the deeper inner work to bring our self-worth in line with our desired net worth. Keep working through the steps in this book, and you'll see what I'm talking about. Then, you'll *really* have your purse strings in your hands . . . instead of that new outfit you bought compulsively, only to feel guilty about it later. (Yuck! I know—been there, done that.)

The Past Could Be Holding the Purse Strings

Sometimes, it's the past that has a tight hold on our purse strings. Earlier in the chapter, you read about Beth. Yes, she relinquished control of the purse strings to her husband, but why? All you have to do is know her history to understand. Beth's mother grew up in an orphanage. Once she was of age, she married a man who was from a poor family—but had big dreams and lots of ambition.

This man—Beth's dad—was an alcoholic. Her mother worked overtime at minimum wage jobs just to keep a roof over their heads. "There was always a threat that the roof wouldn't be there," Beth recalls. "We were always months behind on the mortgage. Once, the sheriff's department had the house on the auction block. Fifteen minutes before it was to be sold, I had to rush in with a check from my uncle. The gas was sometimes shut off. I started working at age 16 to save for college, but I wound up giving all my money to my mom to pay her debts."

When Beth entered adulthood, these patterns from her past followed her. Starving for love, she got married "out of sheer loneliness and pressure from his family," she says. Not having to worry about the money or take care of it was a relief in many ways, but that relief came at a great cost. It wasn't until she found out that her husband was having an affair that she was able to finally cut herself loose from the marriage in spite of her financial fears.

Today, after living on the divorce settlement for years, Beth is working toward creating a living for herself. She's still struggling to make money while following her dreams, but she continues to work on her belief that it's possible to make a living doing what she loves. And most importantly, she's taken hold of her own purse strings.

Even if you're solely responsible for your finances, you could be controlled by the past. Early ideas about what money means can easily get in the way of your financial situation. Maybe you're locked in behaviors similar to your parents, even if you know those habits are dysfunctional. Or perhaps you're rebelling against the way your parents handled finances. You might hear your father's or mother's voice when you want to make a big purchase or try a new profession: "That's too expensive," or "You'll never be able to do that!"

In the next chapter, we'll explore beliefs from our past that control us—beliefs like "the world is not an abundant place, so I'm forced to be frugal" and "I don't understand anything about money, so I have to let my husband handle it" and "I don't have the skills to make any money, so it's up to him to bring home the bacon." These beliefs cause us to feel that we have to relinquish control of our purse strings to someone . . . or *something*.

EXERCISE #5: *WHAT* CONTROLS YOUR PURSE STRINGS?

Whether you're single or married, whether or not there's anyone else in your life who controls your purse strings, answer the questions in this exercise. They'll help you see where you've let your emotions and fears pull the strings.

1. Do you feel guilty if you spend money on yourself? If so, why?

2. Do you spend money on others as a way of earning their love?

3. Do you try to control or manipulate anyone with money? If so, how do you do it?

4. Does the voice of a parent or other authority figure rise up when you're making a purchase, paying bills, or looking at your finances? Whose voice do you hear, and what does he or she say?

5. Do you think something from your past is controlling your purse strings in some way? If so, how?

6. If you're the one in control of the money, do you feel a lot of anxiety about your finances?

Get Ready to Be One of the Lucky Ones

If you're single and making all your own money, it could be hard to figure out where you might have relinquished your purse strings. If that's the case, don't worry. The next steps will help you uncover beliefs and patterns that will give you new insights.

If you've discovered that you hold few purse strings in your life, take heart. By reading this book and working through the exercises, you're already making gradual, but important shifts toward greater self-worth . . . and that will give you back more financial power.

Few people have a clear, balanced relationship with money. Most of us have a person or beliefs controlling our finances in one way or another. If you continue with the remaining steps, however, you'll be one of the lucky ones. You'll learn to see your own destructive patterns at play. You'll start making conscious decisions to change them. The point is to let your purse strings be run by the adult part of you, today, from as clear and free a place as you can muster.

EXERCISE #6: WHAT WOULD IT MEAN TO HOLD YOUR OWN PURSE STRINGS?

What would it mean for you to hold your own purse strings? For now, just define it. As I said earlier in the chapter, it isn't time to take action yet! Remember, if you take action before you're ready, you'll likely perpetuate the same patterns you've been running up against until now. In many ways, these possibilities counteract the answers you gave in Exercise #2 in Step One, when you wrote down what you hide from. For example, if you hide from your finances by putting off paying bills, one way to hold your own purse strings might be paying your bills right away.

As you read each of the following actions someone *might* take as they regain control of their finances, notice what your comfort level is with each one. Which ones might help you feel like you were holding your own purse strings? Which ones feel scary, impossible, or out of reach? Again, don't take any action now—just notice what you feel.

1. Get a "Me Account" (a bank account outside of joint finances with your spouse or other party).

2. Make some of your own money.

3. Open a savings account and make a commitment to put a certain amount in it weekly or monthly.

4. Choose a financial goal and start saving toward it.

5. Create an agreement with your spouse regarding having your own money.

6. Develop marketable skills toward a job.

7. Look for a job.

8. Consult a financial advisor.

9. Open an IRA.

10. Pay bills as soon as they come in.

11. Balance your checkbook regularly.

12. Keep track of what you spend every day.

13. Make a commitment not to use credit cards.

14. Pay off your credit card balances every month.

15. Pay down your debt a certain amount every week or month.

16. Contribute a certain amount to your retirement fund every year.

17. Make a commitment not to use overdraft protection, except in an emergency. (In this case, make a list of what you consider an emergency, and make a commitment to stick to that list and only that list.)

18. Give up excuses for spending on things that aren't important.

19. Buy something for yourself every month as a pure celebration of *you*.

20. Make a commitment to no longer shop as a way to avoid your feelings.

21. Identify what old beliefs are running your financial decisions. (We will work more on this in the next three chapters.)

Add your own statements of financial control:

1. _____

2. _____

3. _____

4. _____

5. _____

6. _____

Affirm Your Worth

*"I'm worthy of holding my own purse strings
and taking control of my finances."*

TAKE INVENTORY OF YOUR BELIEFS

When I was two years old, my six-year-old brother died. Since birth, he had been severely impaired to the point of incapacitation. Even though I was a small child, I was aware that my parents needed to cater to his needs more than mine. So at that young age, I made the decision that his needs were far more pressing than mine. In fact, some part of me decided my own needs were unimportant.

That experience left a number of imprints on me. I grew up believing that I'd better be independent and self-sufficient—or else. I'd better not need anything from anyone, because no one would be there to take care of me. I've lived most of my life based on that belief, as though it were a fact.

My parents, of course, *did* take care of me. They took such good care of my financial needs while I was growing up that they paid for both my college and graduate school education. My belief didn't hold water, but I still couldn't shake it. It was developed when I was too young to understand what was going on. It had been imprinted on my psyche at such a deep level that it had become a part of my reality.

Thanks to the belief that no one would take care of me, the only way I could feel safe was to be entirely self-sufficient. If I ever needed anyone, I felt I was destined to be devastated.

So after grad school, I made damn sure that I was never financially dependent on another person again. As I said in the last chapter, I thought this meant I was holding the purse strings . . . and it certainly looked like I was. But it was really this belief, formed early in my childhood, that was running the show.

What I learned from that experience is this: *The amount of money we make and how we relate to money is a result of the beliefs we carry—both our beliefs about money and our beliefs about our own self-worth.* This is the most important piece of information you'll read in this book! Your beliefs are everything. That's why Step Three is a core part of this process: *Take Inventory of Your Beliefs.*

Through the stories and exercises that follow, you'll discover which beliefs might be inhibiting your sense of self-worth, preventing you from having as much money as you need, stopping you from taking control of your finances, or blocking a feeling of ease about money.

Remember: Some of the beliefs that affect our finances "don't have much to do with finances at all." Our net worth and our self-worth are often intertwined, and our relationship to money is often an emotional one. As one of my clients, Penny, says, "It's all about money, and yet it isn't about money at all."

What's a Belief?

First, let's get absolutely clear on what I mean by "belief." A belief is *a long-held idea about how the world works and our role within it.* We all go through our lives as though our beliefs are facts. Mine was "no one will ever take care of me." If there's one important takeaway from this chapter, it's that a belief and a fact are two different things.

A fact is something that can be objectively proven. For example, it's a fact that I'm a woman. It is *not* a fact that I'm incapable of having enough money to live an abundant life . . . but I could easily have grown up believing that to be a fact.

Families often hold beliefs that are passed down from generation to generation. My client Evelyn's father always said, "There's nothing worse than a rich woman." Obviously, this belief made an impression on Evelyn! Not surprisingly, she's had difficulty accumulating any wealth. On an unconscious level, she certainly didn't want to do anything to become "that" woman. In her young mind, to be wealthy would mean becoming someone her father wouldn't like. If that meant she has to struggle financially, so be it. As a result, her worth as a woman became entangled with her financial future. Can you see how our beliefs about self-worth and our beliefs about money can become a confusing knot in our young psyches? That knot stays bound inside us unless we consciously decide to untie it.

We've already seen how our beliefs about our self-worth can affect our beliefs about money. Our beliefs about money can also affect our self-worth. It's a vicious circle that closes in on itself and doesn't improve until we break the cycle by changing our beliefs. If you grew up in a family that struggled to make ends meet, for example, you might believe you're incapable of having more. There are lots of talented people who never surpassed the circumstances of their family simply because they didn't believe it was possible. Generations of families have struggled financially, often because of nothing more than limiting beliefs.

Marlene and Sheila both grew up in families that suffered from poverty consciousness—a belief that there will never be enough. For some people, this mind-set continues even after they start to make more money—like the millionaire who clips coupons.

Marlene's family's poverty consciousness had a profound effect on her. Constantly struggling financially, her parents shopped at discount stores and bought generic brands almost exclusively in order to save as many bucks as they could. When Marlene began to work on her self-worth and beliefs about money, she discovered that her family's habits had created some very limiting beliefs of hers: "I don't deserve nice things," and "I can't afford anything but bargain-basement stuff."

As a result of these beliefs, Marlene continued to troll dollar stores and Goodwill, buying polyester towels and fake leather handbags—even after she was making enough money to afford higher quality. It was only when she became aware of her limiting beliefs that she was able to beat the poverty consciousness habit she had learned at home. Now, she's happy to not only be able to afford, but to believe she deserves, leather handbags and Egyptian cotton towels and sheets.

In Sheila's case, her mother actually repeatedly used the words "not enough" regarding the family's money situation. "I remember my father used to give my mother the cash from his paycheck on Fridays, and she would stand at the counter and count it with such frustration. I would ask her how much was there, and the answer was always the same— 'Not enough.'"

Sheila's mother struggled to raise five children, largely on her own, and money was always tight. As Sheila got older, this belief of "not enough" stuck with her. "No matter how much I worked, my paycheck seemed to be gone before I got it."

These limiting beliefs that we develop as a result of our dysfunctional family patterns can program the path of our lives—sort of like blueprints. It's up to us as conscious adults to create new blueprints for ourselves based on facts and possibilities, not the beliefs we developed in childhood.

Why is it so hard to let go of limiting family patterns? Most of us grow up believing that all families function the same way ours did. We have no frame of reference for anything else, so we think our beliefs are an accurate reflection of the world at large.

In truth, families are like insular communities. Each has its own operating system. If you speak to others, you'll discover that their families operated under an entirely different set of beliefs, which they, too, believed to be fact.

If you gathered a group of people and asked them to share their beliefs about money, you would get a lot of differing opinions. One person might say, "Rich people are unhappy." Another would say, "Wealth brings happiness." There's no way both of these statements can be objective fact—they're direct opposites. But each of those people is living as if their belief is the absolute truth. This is how we keep ourselves stuck in limitation, which prevents us from living the lives we really want!

Are you ready to discover some of your own limiting beliefs?

EXERCISE #7: MONEY MESSAGES

This exercise has two parts. Part 1 is a meditation, so you will need time and space to be quiet for at least 20 minutes. For Part 2 of this exercise, you'll need your paper, journal, or computer/tablet to record your answers as usual.

Part 1: *First, let's try a meditation to dig deeper and uncover more about beliefs you formed in childhood about money and your self-worth.*

Since this is a meditation, you'll want to close your eyes rather than read as you go through it. So please go to www .nancylevin.com—where I've posted an audio recording of this meditation—and let me guide you through it.

If you can't go to the website, please read the meditation from start to finish before following the directions. Then, go ahead and close your eyes, and try to remember the questions as best you can. It works best if you don't open your eyes and read again for each portion. If you think you'll have trouble remembering, try recording yourself reading the meditation, and play it with your eyes closed.

1. Take several breaths before beginning, and relax each part of your body, starting with your feet. Then, gradually move up your legs, hips, belly, chest, back, arms, neck, and head until you feel fully relaxed.

2. When you're ready, with your eyes closed, ask yourself this question: "What's the loudest message I'm receiving now about money?" Then, just listen for the message. When you hear it, let yourself remember when you first heard that message. Do you know whose voice gave you that message? Was it a parent?

3. Then take another deep breath, and drop down into an even deeper relaxed state. Ask yourself: "What is my first memory about money?" Allow any pictures to come to you. Maybe it's the first time you understood there was a thing called money.

4. Now, take another deep breath, and drop even deeper into a relaxed state. Ask to remember a scene in which your parents dealt with money in some way. How did they handle it?

5. Then, open your eyes and take notes about what you heard and saw. Write down your loudest message about money and what you remembered about your first money memory.

6. Write down what you saw in the scene with your parents. How did they deal with money? What did they say about it?

7. Read what you wrote down from your meditation experience. What beliefs do you think you developed as a result of what you remembered? Write them down, even if you aren't sure about them.

Part 2: *Now that you've opened the door to remembering some of the financial habits within your family, it's time to go back and uncover more of the beliefs they may have instilled in you. Ask yourself the following questions, and write down your answers.*

1. Did your mother and father overspend . . . or penny-pinch? Think back about what this taught you about money.

2. If your parents fought about money, what specifically did they fight about? If your parents didn't talk about money, how did that impact you?

3. Did your parents complain or worry about money a lot? What kinds of things did they say to express their financial worries?

4. Where did your family shop and go out to eat? What do these places say about your parents' beliefs about money?

5. Were you given an allowance? Was anything said about the allowance, how you were supposed to spend it or save it, etc.?

6. Did your parents ever make you feel guilty about the amount of money you cost them?

7. Did your parents ever complain about school expenses or items you asked them for?

8. If you planned to go to college, was it a source of stress for you and your parents from a financial perspective? Did your parents have a college fund for you? Were they afraid there wouldn't be enough money to send you to college? Could you not go to college because your family couldn't afford it?

Go back and read your answers to the questions in this exercise. Make a list of the beliefs you think you developed as a result of these experiences, habits, and patterns within your family.

Next, go back and review your "money myth" from Exercise #1. Can you find additional limiting beliefs in your answers to those questions? If so, add them to your list. Write down at least five to ten beliefs you developed.

Shadow Beliefs

Was the previous exercise difficult for you? If so, take heart. It isn't always easy to discover your beliefs. Because they were formed when we were so young, they often hide out in the unconscious. My mentor, Debbie Ford, coined the term "shadow beliefs" because these beliefs live outside of our conscious awareness. That's why we relate to them as facts.

When emotionally charged events happened to us as children, they felt overwhelming to our little systems. We were simply too young to understand those events with any maturity or objectivity, so we drew the only conclusions we could. That's what happened to me when I decided that my needs were unimportant because, tragically, my brother needed so much attention. We're so suggestible when we're young, and we have little experience to weigh our conclusions against. Our little brains assign meaning to these events and draw conclusions about ourselves, others, and the world that may or may not be accurate. Yet we grow up relating to our conclusions as absolute truths.

For example, if we reach out for love from a parent and are slapped away, we might formulate the belief that love isn't available to us. As a result, we might not bother to look for love in our lives. Even though we've forgotten that we formed a belief that love isn't available to us, our behavior will be driven by this hidden belief. Having low expectations would understandably feel safer than reaching out and possibly getting slapped away again. If we don't go for it, we can spare ourselves ever feeling that awful rejection again.

What we don't realize when we make these decisions so young is that we're consigning ourselves to lives of pain. In this example, the pain would be lack of love and loneliness. When we become adults, we might push people away without awareness and wonder why no one loves us. It's a heartbreaking scenario, but it isn't uncommon.

Another of the beliefs I formed in my mind when my brother died was "If I'm imperfect, I will die." So I ran fast and hard in my life, trying desperately to be perfect at all costs. I didn't know why; I just knew that somehow, my life depended on being perfect. If you've read my book *Jump . . . And Your Life*

Will Appear, you know all about my perfectionism. I worked myself to exhaustion over it.

So why don't we form shadow beliefs around more of the good stuff that happened to us in our families and in our past? Why do we accentuate the negative? Why does our programming get designed around our pain and suffering— rather than our praise and triumphs?

Well, it isn't that we aren't influenced by the positive— of course we are! Those of us lucky enough to have positive childhood experiences tend to have less to heal than those who grew up in seriously abusive situations. But regardless of what we went through in childhood, we're hardwired to look for ways to be safe. This means that the moments when we're hurt or scared are the ones that put us on high alert. These are the experiences we feel we have to watch out for. The meaning we ascribe to such events takes on special impor- tance, because those were the moments we had to *survive*. After all, we were vulnerable little kids when those beliefs were formed. We didn't have the ability to protect ourselves. So we braced against hurt, trying to prepare for the next attack—be it real or perceived.

For example, Lauren had an experience as a child in which all the wealth in her family evaporated. Like my expe- rience with my brother, this was a traumatic event for Lauren that was pivotal in her young life. "It made me feel like, 'Why bother trying to protect your money for the future if some- one's going to take it from you?'" she says. This shadow belief has prevented her from ever saving any money. She's afraid to put money away because she believes she'll be a victim of theft. This, of course, is a fearful belief, not a fact, and it keeps her stuck in limiting financial behaviors. With the awareness that this belief is untrue, Lauren can begin to dismantle and replace it with a new belief that allows her to "reprogram" her thinking and prepare for a better financial future.

Our young minds are actually like little computers, and we do become programmed by our shadow beliefs. The beliefs that develop during our formative years become like our operating system. Our behaviors are the functions of that operating system. We can't perform functions that are outside of the system's abilities . . . not unless we reprogram the system itself.

My client Alicia is another example of how a traumatic experience at a young age can create a long-held limiting belief. She was held back in first grade because she struggled to keep up. Her family and friends teased her about it, laughing and saying things like, "What happened? Did you color outside the lines?" When she was first learning to spell her name, she got it wrong and was even given a nickname based on her mistake. She giggled when people teased her, but she was so deeply wounded by their words that she remembers crying herself to sleep at night for a long time.

The belief she formulated as a result was "I'm stupid," and she has lived her life based on that belief . . . as if it were a fact. She fights it, of course, and she's even proven it wrong numerous times. She went on to make the honor roll in high school and even earn a Ph.D. in mathematics! But the belief that she's dumb is persistent—as shadow beliefs usually are—and it rises up to haunt her whenever she doesn't succeed as much as she hoped to.

She discovered through our work together that her biggest shadow belief around her finances was that she wasn't smart enough to make, in her words, "real money." It was an "aha!" moment for Alicia. Armed with the awareness about her negative belief, she can now work on replacing it with a more positive one that reflects the reality of her intelligence.

Coming up at the end of the chapter, you'll try some of the same exercises as Alicia to change your beliefs. But first, let's see if we can bring even more of your own beliefs out of the "shadows."

Which of These Beliefs Sound Familiar?

To help you uncover more of your shadow beliefs, my clients and I have gathered some of our most common beliefs about money, many of which are entangled with self-worth issues. Make note of the ones you share, adding them to your beliefs list from Exercise #7. Note how contradictory some of them are: For example, "Poor people are powerless," and "Poor people are happier." This only proves that they're beliefs, not facts!

1. I don't make enough money to save anything.

2. I have to work hard to make any money.

3. I couldn't make enough money if I tried.

4. I will always struggle.

5. I can't afford to pay full price for anything.

6. Everything I want is too expensive.

7. If I take a financial risk, I'll lose everything.

8. I'm too old; I've been out of the workforce for too long.

9. I have no skills.

10. I can't afford to go back to school.

11. Without a higher education, I'm not qualified/worthy enough to make more money than I make now.

12. Luxuries are for other people.

13. Wealthy people got their money dishonestly.

14. Luxuries are selfish.

15. It's selfish to think about my own wants and desires. My kids'/husband's/clients' needs are more important than mine.

16. I don't trust my desires. My parents dreamed big, and it all went to hell.

17. If I make a lot of money, I'll just be irresponsible and lose it all.

18. You can't make money doing what you love.

19. People want to take all my money.

20. People with money are greedy.

21. People without much money don't work hard enough and are irresponsible.

22. You have to have money to make money.

23. My happiness depends on the amount of money I have in my bank account.

24. If I make a lot of money, I'll finally be happy and at peace.

25. I don't deserve the money I have because I didn't work for it.

Secrets, Lies, and Judgments

Ruth says her family has always kept all sorts of secrets about money. "I think there's a lot of dishonesty around money in my family—how much something costs, how much one has or makes, how much debt one is in, what money is being spent on. My sister judges me for the ways I choose to spend my money." This secrecy taught Ruth that money was something to hide, be ashamed of, or be frightened about.

It also created beliefs in her that self-worth and money are linked . . . and not in a good way. How many people do you know who think they aren't worthy unless they make a certain amount of money? Given that, might they feel the need to embellish or stretch the truth about their financial situation? But lying about how much we make is a direct result of low self-worth. We don't feel the need to pretend to be better off than we are unless we believe that the truth isn't good enough. We're worried others will judge us as "less than" because our bank accounts are . . . well, "less than"—at least in our perception. But if someone else judges us based on how much money we make, that says more about their values than it does about us, doesn't it?

Still, many of us carry the belief that others will look down on us if we don't make "enough" money. Underlying that fear is our own belief that our self-worth is dependent upon our income. And that's a prime reason many of us are secretive about how much we make. Or we pretend to make more than we do in the hope that others will see us the way we want to see ourselves. In fact, a lot of people overspend in order to look the part of someone who has more money. To keep up appearances, they buy clothes or drive a car or take vacations they can't really afford.

This is one of the ways shame comes into play with our belief system. If we believe we aren't worthy without a certain income, we'll feel shame if we don't maintain that income. As you'll learn in Step Six, however, self-worth is at its height when it's unconditional. In other words, you're worthy regardless of your bank balance!

Secrecy about money is quite common in families, especially between siblings, and between parents and adult children. We're secretive about money for a variety of reasons. Usually, it's a result of one of the following: (1) we feel we have to protect our money from others, or (2) we feel we're going to be judged for our income or money decisions. When a hoarder in a family meets an overspender, for example, watch out! There can be a lot of judgments on both sides. Sometimes, family members have certain ideas about how money should be handled and insist that we do it their way—even if we disagree.

In some cases, of course, secrecy isn't a bad thing. As Cassidy has worked on her self-worth and grown her net worth, the other members of her family have continued to struggle financially. They haven't done the kind of self-worth work Cassidy is doing. So to avoid family members constantly asking for handouts, as has happened in the past, Cassidy has chosen to keep her income private.

We're under no obligation to disclose our personal finances to anyone, except the IRS! When you can't keep a financial decision private, stand your ground about the choices you make. When Michele from the Introduction moved to Hawaii, she was worried about being judged by her family. Her sister is struggling, and her father would no doubt think it was impetuous. She couldn't hide where she was living, so she had to work on her beliefs and self-worth issues until she knew she was worthy of making her own decisions.

Her family's judgments still make her uncomfortable, but Michele is now strong in her self-worth. She knows she has every right to choose what she wants for her life, regardless of what anyone else thinks about it. And their judgments no longer cause her sense of worthiness to waver.

Secrecy is only a problem if it comes from low self-worth, or when we hide our financial decisions from people who have a personal stake.

Did your family's habits around secrets and lies create any unconscious limiting beliefs for you? Let's see.

EXERCISE #8: SECRETS, LIES, AND JUDGMENTS

These questions are about the secrets, lies, and judgments you may have experienced in or inherited from your family. After answering them you'll then try to excavate the beliefs that you developed as a result. Record your answers to each question.

1. To your knowledge, did your parents keep secrets or tell lies about money? If so, did they keep the secrets from or lie to (1) you, (2) each other, (3) other family members, or (4) their friends? If so, why did they lie or keep secrets?

2. Have you ever kept a secret or lied about money? If so, who did you keep the secret from or lie to? Why did you feel the need to keep the secret or lie? What would have happened if the other person or people had learned the truth? If you did tell the truth, or they found out, what was the consequence? What did you learn from the situation?

3. To your knowledge, were your parents ever judged by family members or friends for their income, spending habits, or saving habits? If so, who judged them? What were the judgments about? Do you think the judgments were justified? How did your parents feel about the judgments?

4. Did your parents ever express judgments of others about money issues? If so, who did they judge? What was the nature of their judgments? Do you think the judgments were justified?

5. Have you ever been judged by a family member for your income, spending habits, or savings habits? If so, who judged you? What were the judgments about? Do you think the judgments were justified? How have you felt about these judgments?

6. Have you ever judged a family member for their income, spending habits, or saving habits? What were the judgments about? Do you think the judgments were justified? In retrospect, how could you have handled the situation better?

7. Review your answers to the previous questions. What beliefs do you think you developed as a result of those experiences? For example, when she was a kid, Anne's father used to slip $20 to her and tell her not to say anything to her mother. She always felt loved when he did this. As a result, she developed a belief that money equals love.

The Magnetism of Beliefs

One of the reasons beliefs are so effective in dictating our reality is that they act as magnets. They cause us to draw toward us the people and circumstances that seem to confirm them as truth. After all, there's nothing the ego loves more than being right. For example, Rose had a belief that she was "no good with money." So she took a finance course that was much too advanced for her and couldn't keep up with the lessons. She then used that as proof that she's indeed "no good with money." Later, when she bought some stock that didn't do well, her ex-husband said, "You just have no money sense, do you?" He even laughed when he said it, but there was nothing funny about it for Rose. It just confirmed the negative belief she had always had.

When she took the time to explore the origins of her beliefs, she realized that she had "borrowed" hers from her mother. Her mom had also felt she was "no good" with money. When Rose was able to separate fact from belief, she reminded herself that there was no reason she couldn't learn to be "good with money." She took a beginning finance course that was more appropriate for her. It wasn't long before she was able to take the more advanced course. As a result, she was able to not only boost her self-worth but also grow her net worth.

Besides energetically attracting experiences that confirm our beliefs, we also interpret everything through the filter of those beliefs. We might even go so far as to dismiss something that doesn't fit a belief. How many times have you brushed off a compliment and considered it irrelevant? That's only because it didn't fit with your belief about your own self-worth.

Let's say you have a fundamental belief that you aren't intelligent. Any time you make a mistake, your belief is confirmed. You tell yourself it's just more proof you aren't intelligent. If, on the other hand, you believe you're smart, you'll probably brush it off when you make a mistake. After all, nobody's right all the time. You take it as a learning experience rather than some indication of your intelligence.

Similarly, if you believe all "rich" people are selfish, you'll not only attract situations that prove your belief, but you'll *interpret your experiences* based on that belief. You might meet someone who has what you consider to be a lot of money, and you'll view their behavior as selfish. If you found out more about that person, you might discover that they aren't selfish at all. They only appeared to be so because you were interpreting their behavior through the filter of your belief. You've probably had the experience of meeting someone and making a snap judgment. Later, when you met the person again, you realized that your initial judgment was wrong. That's how belief filters get in our way.

When we become aware of our beliefs or take the plunge to act in spite of them, we have the opportunity to prove them wrong. I'm sure if you review your past, you'll find things you once thought were fact that have since been proven to be nothing more than misguided beliefs.

The work is to become aware of our beliefs—so we can begin to objectively evaluate the facts. With time, we begin to disengage from any beliefs that are no longer serving us. We can then consciously choose new, empowering beliefs that serve us in the present and draw different people and circumstances into our world.

Here's an example of how this worked in my own life. I believed that I had to buy love in relationships, so I attracted a man into my life who wanted someone to take care of him.

By working through the steps in this book, I was able to alter that belief until I knew I was worthy of love for who I am and not what I do or give. That new belief allowed me to attract a healthier relationship with someone who doesn't expect me to support him. I can give freely to him without feeling that I have to "earn" his love.

As we let go of limiting beliefs, our self-worth increases. As a result, we become magnetic to more of what we want—rather than what we don't want. For example, someone might have a pattern of attracting jobs where they aren't respected. The more they increase their self-worth by replacing old beliefs, the better chance they'll have of attracting a job in which the respect they receive matches their stronger self-worth.

Again, these changes don't happen overnight. But during the transition from leaving behind our old beliefs and creating new ones, we start to notice our patterns. For example, while the new beliefs are in the process of becoming "installed" to upgrade our operating system, we become more aware of when we misinterpret situations based on our old beliefs. We catch ourselves in the act of thinking in limited ways. Or we notice ourselves attracting a situation that's similar to one we attracted in the past—and we make a conscious choice *not* to engage in the old pattern. This is how change happens, and how our beliefs cease to have power over us.

Is Money the Root of All Evil?

That old adage about money and evil is a problem for those of us who want to open to the flow of more money in our lives. "Money is bad" is a pervasive belief that originated in the New Testament of the Bible. There's a verse (Timothy 6:10) that's often quoted as "money is the root of all evil," but the actual translation is more accurate as "*love* of money is the root of all evil." Remember that money is nothing but a physical representation of life energy. It's been infused into form, coming into our lives as paper bills or metal coins. That's it. Money is only as "good" or "evil" as we believe it to be.

On your list of beliefs, were there any beliefs about the wealthy? One of my clients says, "My dad spoke badly about wealthy people. He acted as if they had done something wrong and didn't deserve or appreciate what they had. Looking back, I can see he was also jealous. He *wanted* their wealth."

Another client says, "I was taught, and believed for many years, that people who had money had acquired it by nefarious means. But I've encountered many people who have made their money doing wonderful work in the world, and that's the path I'm seeking—making abundant money while inspiring the world. But some of that old judgment still creeps in."

Articles about economic inequality and the wealthiest one percent are all over the news these days. These stories would lead us to believe that all so-called wealthy people are heartless and greedy. Can that possibly be true? Of course not! But as long as that belief remains in our psyche, a part of us will resist joining their ranks. If you became one of the one percent, it doesn't mean you would suddenly turn into an awful person. If you wanted to be charitable, think of all the good you could do in the world!

So if "money is the root of all evil" is one of your beliefs, it's time to put that one to rest for good! In the last exercise of the chapter, you can work with that belief and create a new one. As long as this belief is in place in your unconscious, you'll struggle to create the financial ease you desire.

Cultural Beliefs

While most of our beliefs are instilled in us during childhood, some of them come from the culture at large. Psychologist Carl Jung came up with the term "collective unconscious," which refers to beliefs in our unconscious mind that are shared by all humankind. These beliefs can impact the whole marketplace.

For example, when the media tells us that the economy is in a terrible state, a large number of us add that information to the collective unconscious and go about our lives attracting circumstances to substantiate that belief. But even when we're in a "down" economy, plenty of people continue to thrive, unaffected by market fluctuations. Not everybody buys into the cultural belief.

Another current cultural belief is "There isn't enough." Most human beings on the planet believe, falsely, that there's a finite amount of money, success, love, and good fortune. Like a zero-sum game, we believe that if we have it, others won't. Again, money is energy! We can transform energy if we choose.

That's not to say there aren't wealthy people who've obtained their money through dishonest means. People at all income levels steal, embezzle, and break the law all the time. But once we're able to zoom out and look at our financial choices from the perspective of shadow beliefs, a certain compassion sets in. Anyone who's lying or stealing is no doubt doing so out of their own shadow beliefs, based in pain and fear. Not that justice shouldn't be applied—we're all responsible for maintaining integrity, regardless of the unconscious forces that move us. But what I want to underscore is that the behavior of the wealthy has *nothing* to do with the amount of money available in the world.

Another belief that gets in the way for many people goes something like "What right do I have to be wealthy when so many people are suffering?" This harkens back to the Marianne Williamson quote from Step One, about our fear of being as big as we actually are. Let me repeat: Keeping ourselves down doesn't help other people avoid suffering. Holding a belief like this can cause us to unconsciously deplete our resources in an effort to create a level playing field for all. If someone else has less than we have, we can assume it's the result of shadow beliefs—either personal or cultural, or some combination of both. Working toward cultural changes to make the playing field more equal is a responsibility I take seriously. But choosing poverty because wealth is "unfair" is not going to help any of us create better lives.

The belief that it's not okay to have money can be especially powerful if someone in our own family is less fortunate than we are. Our cultural beliefs and childhood beliefs may become enmeshed. Many of us hold the belief that we can't have more than our siblings or our parents or others in our family. I have to remind my clients all the time that they're not responsible for others' poor money management. Moreover, they have every right to enjoy the fruits of the talents and skills that allow them to make more money than others. Still, surpassing our parents financially is a difficult hurdle and requires a great deal of belief in ourselves. If you've managed to do that, it's a big accomplishment.

Nevertheless, when we make more money than our family of origin, we stop belonging to the family in a fundamental way. It creates a form of separation, and that naturally leads to some feelings of guilt. I have found that self-talk is the best defense against these feelings. We can remind ourselves that we're not responsible for others. Still, twinges of guilt may come up from time to time. The important thing is to never let guilt become an excuse to hold ourselves back from reaching our full potential. I'd certainly be resentful if I felt the need to make less money just to stay in sync with my family.

If you're in a position to help out a member of your family or a friend because it feels balanced and heartfelt to do so, by all means, give. Just ask whether you're giving out of a sense of guilt or obligation. If so, it's a tainted gift that will eventually lead to resentment. When you feel the impulse to give to someone else, check in with yourself: Do I feel joyful and expansive about giving, or do I feel contracted and guilty? Does my body feel relaxed or tense? Your body is the barometer of your truth.

We carry beliefs that originated in our individual childhoods, and we carry cultural beliefs from the collective unconscious. That may feel like a double whammy, but no matter how pervasive these beliefs seem to be, they are *not* carved in stone! Trust me, you've already changed a lot of beliefs throughout your life, especially on the road from childhood to adulthood. So you can do it again. Let's start right now!

EXERCISE #9: PROVE YOUR BELIEFS WRONG

Part 1: *Now that you know many of your shadow beliefs, we're going to see which ones you can prove wrong. This exercise has a Part 2, in which you'll create a new, empowering belief to replace each of the limiting beliefs.*

1. Draw two vertical lines on a piece of paper, or create three columns on your screen.

    Label the left column "Old Belief."

    Label the middle column "Counter-Example."

    Label the right column "New Belief."

2. Look at the beliefs you wrote down in the first two
    exercises of this chapter. Choose the five beliefs that
    you feel are currently the most damaging. Write down
    each of these five beliefs in the "Old Belief" column,
    drawing a horizontal line under each one across all of
    the columns.

Old Belief	Counter-Example	New Belief
1. Nobody loves their job.		
2.		
3.		
4.		
5.		

3. Looking at each belief in turn, ask yourself if there's ever
    been a counter-example to that belief. Can you come
    up with a time in your life when each of these beliefs
    was proven untrue? For example, let's say you've al-
    ways held the belief "Nobody loves their job." Well,
    you're reading a book right now by someone who ab-
    solutely *loves* her job! I would do it for free. So you
    can write in the middle column, "Nancy Levin loves
    her job." What about "Everything I want is too expen-
    sive"? Surely there's something you've wanted in your
    life that you've been able to afford. In the middle col-
    umn next to that belief, write down something you
    really wanted that you were able to buy. Do this for
    each belief in your left column. If you have more than
    one counter-example, write them all down.

Old Belief	Counter-Example	New Belief
1. Nobody loves their job.	Nancy Levin loves her job!	
2.		
3.		
4.		
5.		

4. If you come upon a belief for which you have no counter-example, put a star in the second column. As you work through the rest of the book, you'll likely find one. Let's say you hold the belief "I have no marketable skills." Even if you feel you haven't disproved that belief up to now, all you have to do is study something that's marketable. By the time you're finished with this book, you'll be able to go back to your beliefs list and cross many of them off, one by one.

Part 2: *Next, let's create new beliefs that feel empowering and positive.*

Take a look at the left-hand column again. Read each belief, and create a new belief to replace the old one. Write your new belief in the third column on the right. For example, if your belief is "I don't have any skills," the new belief might be "I have plenty of skills and talents that I can offer in the marketplace," or "I can learn new skills that will be profitable in the marketplace."

Old Belief	Counter-Example	New Belief
1. Nobody loves their job.	Nancy Levin loves her job!	I can make money doing what I love.
2.		
3.		
4.		
5.		

Affirm Your Worth

"My beliefs are in harmony with the life I desire."

TALLY THE COST OF YOUR EXCUSES

Chloe—an author, yoga teacher, and wellness facilitator—struggles with the desire to play on a bigger stage. "My mom was an amazing professional belly dancer. She could have taken over the world! But she chose to teach at the local adult school and dance at private parties until she retired from performing," Chloe says.

"My dad is an amazing baseball coach. He could have coached for professional teams. But he chose to teach his whole career at one high school. He also created his own sports camp, which could be a franchise, but he has chosen to keep it at one. These choices are fine for my parents. They have their path. However, I feel called to reach a bigger audience. Up until recently, I've been following in their footsteps—staying at the local level. I teach classes at some yoga studios around town, and I teach my own life-coaching program. Everyone around my town has my book, and I have a local fan base. But I know I'm meant to take my work to a national level. And every time I think about that, I feel scared. It's out of my comfort zone."

So what's the belief that stands in Chloe's way? "I tell myself if I went bigger, I wouldn't have enough time for my family," she says. And that belief has turned into an *excuse* that keeps her stuck right where she is. Would Chloe *really* not have enough time for her family? Chances are she could find a way to make it work.

Our excuses, like our beliefs, can easily sound like facts. But also like beliefs, they aren't the truth. That's why they're called *excuses*! They are convenient ways of keeping us safe from risk, safe from trying something new . . . but also safely distant from the life we most desire. They limit our options so that we can avoid the scary unknown.

I've certainly been paralyzed by excuses. Remember my story of keeping so much money in a low interest-bearing account that my financial advisor said it was like planting frozen vegetables and expecting them to grow? My excuse was that I "didn't know how" to invest. In truth, I had never bothered to learn . . . until I finally took control with Step Four: *Tally the Cost of Your Excuses.*

What's an Excuse?

Our excuses come in all kinds of sneaky disguises that cause us to think they make a lot of sense. But really, they're very similar to our limiting beliefs. Excuses take our beliefs and run with them. You could say they're just our beliefs in sheep's clothing. When excuses take hold, our self-imposed limitations are no longer just thoughts. Our excuses actually stop us cold and prevent us from moving forward in our lives. They're always based in fear, and their aim is inaction. Even when we use an excuse to take an action like overspending, it's actually *inaction* in another area.

That was the case with Theresa. By exploring her beliefs and excuses, she has come to terms with the fact that she spends money to avoid what she really wants—to leave her job and start over. "My spending pushes my 'quit my job' date, because I don't have any savings to fall back on," she says. She could, instead, spend her energy figuring out how to make a solid move from her current job.

But she hasn't yet because she's *resistant* to what she wants. Resistant because of that fear-of-the-unknown thing we all seem to have.

Yep, excuses are actually just well-packaged resistance. But our resistance also has a lot to do with our self-worth. When we feel worthy, we don't resist what's good for us. We feel we deserve what we want, so we find it much easier to step right over our fears and go for it. That's the blessing of worthiness! If we don't feel we deserve what we want, we let resistance keep us down.

Debbie Ford defined resistance as "an unconscious protective defense mechanism, a programmed reaction rather than a conscious choice." In my case, I avoided learning about my 401(k) plan because I was unconsciously defending myself against looking stupid. Talk about a self-worth problem! Avoidance, disinterest, and inaction were my programmed reactions to this perceived threat. Whenever we choose to fight against or deny something that seems threatening, if we look under the hood, we'll find resistance . . . and under that will be self-worth issues.

Now, like our beliefs, our resistance was put into place for very good reasons—to protect us when we were small and defenseless. Later in life, though, that same resistance protects us from joy and expansiveness, from reaching our potential and fulfillment. We protect ourselves from imagined hurts and defeats, huddling up within a comfort zone that was built for us as children.

In my book *Jump . . . And Your Life Will Appear*, there's a chapter called "Honor Your Resistance." It's true that not all resistance is bad. It's smart to resist anything that isn't good for us. It's when we resist the good and create excuses to hold us back that we unwittingly create exactly what we don't want in life. You may have heard the phrase "what we resist persists"—it's a common adage because it's true.

Honoring your resistance means you don't bulldoze over the parts of you that are afraid. Yet there comes a time when you have to work through the fear and get on with the business of letting the excuses go.

Recognize Your Excuses

"I can't . . ." "I don't know how . . ." "I have to . . ." These are just some of the ways we tend to phrase our excuses.

For example, Vicki says she "can't make it on her own," and she has a whole set of beliefs and excuses to stop herself from taking action. Her financial dependency started by watching her mother, who repeatedly got them into financial jams and was always bailed out by her own parents. As a result, Vicki has become dependent upon her husband and has excuses for staying that way. "I have told myself for a long time that I'm not 'one of those people' who's capable of having a 'normal' nine-to-five job," she says. "I'm not merely incapable, but downright *exempt* from earning a living on my own. I can get self-righteous and see myself as 'above working' somehow. But it also makes me feel bad about myself and makes it hard to spend the money my husband makes. Because I didn't directly earn it, and I can't replenish it once it's gone, I can't spend it how I want."

Diana is stuck in the belief that she has to hoard money in order to feel safe. Her excuse? "I can't spend money, or I'll run out." She even sometimes accepts dinner invitations from people she doesn't like because they'll pay for it. She gives herself another excuse for that: "At least it won't have been me who 'wasted' that money," she says. "This fear of spending costs me moving forward in my life in so many ways."

Noele has a similar fear of lack. She works in customer service and doesn't make a lot of money. Her excuse for not changing her situation is "I can't leave my job because I don't have family to fall back on." Now, I would never tell anyone to blindly quit a job without some safety net in place. But there are a number of ways that someone can begin slowly to move out of unfulfilling circumstances. After our work together on the steps of this process, Noele is taking important steps toward a better career situation.

Erica uses the excuse that she has to wait for something to happen. This excuse has her paralyzed in inaction. "My excuse for not diving more completely into life is that nobody has handed that life to me yet! I'm waiting for someone to tell me what path I should be on, and to give me permission to succeed," she says. Whether we're waiting for an inheritance, for a better job offer, or for "the Universe to provide," we need to remember that waiting for an external sign comes at a cost—just like any other excuse.

For Janice, the excuse "I can't have money" has come about because she believes she won't be loved if she does what she really desires. She has watched her family members make choices that don't allow them to have the money they want. In order to belong, she's done the same and used her family as an excuse to stay small—and have precious little money in the bank. After working the steps, she has come to a realization. "I can still make my choices, make money, have what I want, work toward financial freedom, work toward job flexibility, and not feel guilty if others don't find the same freedom and flexibility in their work and financial lives," she says. "I have to be okay with being me, and be okay with knowing that I can create my own world. I don't have to help everyone else achieve what they say they want when they're not making aligned choices that bring them results." And she can trust that she'll still be loved if she doesn't follow her family's dysfunctional patterns.

When we tell ourselves, "I can't," what we're usually saying is "I won't." Using "can't" allows us to pretend we have no choice but to give in to our excuses. But "can't" is a matter of not having the *skill* to do something, while "won't" is a matter of not having the *will*. If we "can't," it's only because we haven't bothered to develop the skills. In most cases, all we have to do is make the effort. (Okay, if you're hopelessly uncoordinated or over the age of 35, maybe you "can't" ever become an Olympic gymnast. But I'll assume that isn't one of your desires—and you *can* still learn some gymnastics at a lower level!)

The point is that most of the time, we *can*—if only we're *willing* to step past our resistance. It's a choice to give in to fear and what we're resistant to. Try replacing your "I can't" with "I'm resistant to." For example, "I'm resistant to trying to make it on my own." "I'm resistant to spending money." "I'm resistant to leaving my job." "I'm resistant to taking responsibility and doing something for myself." It isn't that we *can't*. It's that our limiting beliefs have caused us to make excuses for not doing what we'd do if we weren't so afraid.

Sometimes, we phrase an "I can't" excuse as "I have to," and we focus on the action we feel compelled to take rather than the action we're avoiding. Fiona had a belief she wasn't safe unless she was accepted by others. That belief became an excuse to overspend on ways to look good. "I have to buy this so that I look good for my job and social life" was really an excuse for not taking action toward boosting her self-worth. Once Fiona became aware that she placed too much importance on her appearance, she could feel worthy without needing to spend so much money on impressing others. She might also eventually find that there's a deeper belief underneath her excuse that causes her to overspend. The deeper inside we dig, the more excuses and beliefs we find. With that awareness, we create more opportunities to change our lives for the better.

I already told you about my excuse: "I don't know how to invest." The "I don't know how" excuse is a common one. How many women have stayed in bad marriages for years based on the excuse that they didn't know how to make money on their own? But honestly, if we don't know how to do something, we can simply *learn how*. It's just another way of saying "I can't" instead of "I will." Thankfully, I've now discovered that I'm perfectly capable of learning how to take care all sorts of things I previously didn't know I could do.

Some of us use the excuse that it will take too long to learn something new, but if we never begin, we never get there. It's okay for learning to be slow . . . as long as we do it. How many of us don't go back to school because "it will take years!" Then, four years down the road, we're in the same situation because we never started.

There's also the "just this once" excuse. It's the same thing we say when we're dieting, right? "Just this once, I'll have a piece of cake. I'll do better tomorrow." When it comes to money matters, we might say, "Just this once, I'll buy this great new iPad. I'll start saving tomorrow."

Our beliefs feed our excuses, but our excuses also feed our beliefs. It's a regular feeding frenzy. Robin says, "I have a pattern of spending money I don't have—jumping into big experiences that cost a lot, or going to the casino with my last $20. All this when I have no savings and live paycheck to paycheck! Seems kind of stupid, right? Well, I'm starting to realize I do it on purpose. Feeling behind on my finances feeds the belief that I'm not that smart, which has always been my excuse for not being wealthy." Like so many of us, Robin used her beliefs and excuses to hold herself back. She believed she wasn't smart, and that became her excuse for not being wealthy. But the real reason? Her spending patterns. Feeling stupid was probably a defense mechanism, keeping Robin from taking risks that she feared wouldn't go well. To the small child within, being "stupid" and "small" felt safer to her than actualizing her full potential.

Megan has a different excuse for overspending. Her father used to say, "Hon, there will always be something that comes up that you're not prepared for. Just when you get ahead, something will happen." His words became a hidden belief in Megan's life that "something will always come up to steal my joy and my freedom." This belief then turned into her overspending excuse. "I think this is probably the reason for my unconscious spending in my early 20s through my mid-40s," she says. "If I was *never* going to have freedom, I might as well enjoy each day and buy whatever I wanted— even if it was beyond my means. I subconsciously decided not to strive for freedom, not to save, and not to pay anything off. Why bother? I'd still never achieve the freedom I so desired." And her excuse has kept her stuck without any savings.

Recently, I saw a funny article called "The Only 31 Things Standing Between You and Your Dreams." It lists many of the typical obstacles that we use as excuses—student loans, the wrong age, not enough education, too many obligations, the wrong location. Seeing them all together was a bit laughable because it showed just how much we get in our own way. Of course, these excuses are not at all funny when they hold us back from the lives we could be leading.

I've heard dozens of excuses like these from my friends and clients (and, yes, myself):

- I can't start my own business because I can only earn money in a salaried job.

- I can't go back to school because I don't have the money.

- I can't learn a new skill because I'm too old.

As you can see, our excuses are the way we reinforce our beliefs. They're how we explain why we don't already have everything we say we want. They're a form of self-sabotage because they give us permission not to try. They're justifications, explanations, and rationalizations. We rationalize our choices and convince ourselves that there are no other options. And the benefit of those excuses is that we get to stay in our comfort zone. That makes sense to the child within, but for the adult, it's a pretty lame benefit, isn't it? Stepping out of our comfort zone and living a full, juicy life—now, *that's* a benefit!

"I've Got No Time"

Like Chloe in the chapter's opening story, we frequently use time as an "I can't" excuse. And time is actually money. If you don't yet have enough time to do what you want, reading this book and going through the steps will help. So congratulations for making the *time* to read!

For Sharon, the excuse was "I can't pursue my first love—acting—because I don't have time." Frequently, she found herself moving from one place to another and using the excuse that "it takes so long to get settled." She followed her fiancé to Texas, where there were few opportunities for actors. "I had to take care of so-and-so, or I had to go do this for somebody else," she says. "But I chose every single one of those things, and I was always operating under the assumption that somehow, everyone else had been given the secret rule book. But that's just an excuse. Nobody else knows how to do it either."

She allowed herself to believe that (1) others made their careers happen via some sort of magic that she didn't have access to, and (2) it was everyone else in her life who prevented her from pursuing the career she wanted. Now, Sharon finds herself with enough time for her career, but it's difficult to let go of the excuses because it means she has to take the risk and the responsibility. Going through the steps to bring her beliefs and excuses into awareness will help, along with increasing her self-worth. As I've said, the more worthy we feel, the less we're willing to use excuses to give up. We know we deserve the best life, and we're willing to take the risk to get it!

How many of your excuses are about not having enough time?

The "What If?" Syndrome

As I said, our excuses are always based in fear. And because our excuses also come out of shadow beliefs that were formed when we were so young, many of them are irrational. They're no more real than the monster we believed was in the closet when we were kids.

These fears keep us locked in worst-case scenarios—or what has been called the "What if?" syndrome. Those of us with this syndrome are plagued by "What if?" questions that keep us from taking positive action. For example, I was so afraid of the "What if I run out of money?" excuse that I held on to funds for years—funds that could have grown into much more had I put them in proper interest-bearing accounts!

Here are some common "What if?" excuses:

- What if I look at my finances and discover that I don't have enough money?
- What if my husband divorces me, and I can't take care of myself?
- What if I never have enough money to retire?
- What if I can't get a job?
- What if I lose my job?
- What if I lose this house that I've put so much time and energy into?
- What if I become disabled?
- What if I end up homeless?

The possibilities for "what ifs" are endless, and it's easy to drive ourselves crazy with such doom-and-gloom stories—most of which are highly unlikely to happen. In fact, there's a good chance *none* of them will happen. Even if one of them comes your way, worrying about it now is probably not going to help you prepare for it. Taking positive action toward healthy self-worth and financial habits might, though!

EXERCISE #10: WHAT DO YOU WANT MOST?

In order to help you figure out how your excuses hold you back, let's discover what might be your most common excuse.

1. Identify what you want most but don't yet have. Think about it for a few minutes. What's your number one desire? Write it down.

2. Now, write down why you don't have whatever it is that you want. What's in the way?

3. This "reason" is your excuse. Write it down. Here's an example: Jolene has wanted to go to Paris for as long as she can remember. Her reason/excuse for never doing it? "I don't have enough money." Actually, when she dug deeper, she discovered that her belief is an absolute that had blocked her from any options: "I'll never have enough money."

4. Now, rephrase your excuse. It helps to start with "I can't." This makes it absolutely clear. For example, Jolene's excuse is: "I can't go to Paris because I don't have enough money." If you struggle to rephrase your excuse, don't worry. The wording isn't nearly as important as identifying it. If you can start your excuse with "I can't," write it down. Otherwise, leave your excuse as you first wrote it down.

5. Now, rephrase your excuse, replacing "I can't" with "I'm resistant to." You can even add "believe" if there's an appropriate spot. In Jolene's example, her excuse "I can't go to Paris because I don't have enough money" becomes "*I'm resistant to going* to Paris because I *believe* I don't have enough money." Again, don't worry so much about how you phrase your excuses. The most important part is to see that it isn't a matter of "can't" but a matter of *resistance.* If you're *willing* to find a way, you *can* almost always get past your resistance and do what you really want to do.

6. "I'm resistant to _____ because I *believe* _____

   _____."

7. Now, imagine that a friend gave you that same excuse. What creative ideas could you come up with to help her find a way around the obstacle? Jolene might say, "If you put even a tiny bit of money away every month,

you'd eventually have enough money to go to Paris. Perhaps you could find a job teaching English there or writing for an English-language newspaper."

8. Look at your excuse again, and review the "What If?" Syndrome section above. Do you have any "what ifs" associated with your excuse? If so, write them down. For Jolene, the "what ifs" included "What if I go to Paris and can't find my way around?" and "What if I spend the money on the trip and have something catastrophic happen that I should have used the money for instead?"

9. For each of your "what ifs," write down the worst-case scenarios. Here's what Jolene wrote: "What if I go to Paris and can't find my way around? I could end up completely lost on the street with no one to help me. I could end up in a dangerous part of town and get raped or kidnapped or killed. I could get hit by a car."

10. Next, look at your worst-case scenario and write down what you could do to avoid these possibilities. Here's what Jolene wrote: "I can always find someone who speaks English to help me. I can take a map with me or use my smartphone to help me find my way. I can ask around until I find someone who has a friend in Paris—someone I can call upon if I run into problems." For her other "what if," Jolene wrote: "What if I spend the money on the trip and have something catastrophic happen that I should have used the money for instead? I can't live my life worrying about possible catastrophes. If I do, I'll never end up living at all. Maybe it's time I go to Paris!"

Truth vs. Excuses

Here's the deal with excuses: They're self-imposed limitations that have nothing to do with reality. Remember that just like our beliefs, our excuses are not facts.

An excuse is usually about the future, while a fact is about the present. "Right now, I don't have enough money in the bank to buy a new car." That's a fact. The excuse might be "I can't buy a car because I don't have the skills to get a better job." That's an excuse based on the belief "I'm too old to learn new skills." The truth is that no matter this person's age, if she just put her mind to it, there's a very good chance she could learn new skills and get a better job. Then, she could eventually buy that new car she wants. But she would have to risk failure to do it, and ultimately, her excuse is resistance to the risk of failure. She hopes to be "excused" from the challenge of doing something that feels scary.

Financial excuses like that one are often circular: "I can't leave my day job because I don't have enough savings, but I don't have time to launch my own business because I'm working all the time." It's the proverbial Catch-22. While it might be difficult to get past these kinds of excuses, it can be done.

Yes, it may appear to be a hard fact that you don't have the savings to support yourself if you quit your job. It may be true that you haven't worked for years, that the job market is tough, or that you don't know how to make it on your own. But none of those obstacles are insurmountable. We live in an infinite universe, where creativity and possibility abound.

To dissolve the cycle of excuses, the first step is to remember that there are *always* options and choices. When we tell ourselves there's only one possible outcome, that means we're not looking at the situation creatively enough.

Let's say you want to leave your marriage, but you haven't worked in over a decade, and you're afraid nobody will hire you. What are the facts here? First, you want to leave. That's an important truth! Second, you haven't worked in a decade—that's also true. But is it true that nobody will hire you? Are you sure? What if you took the next few months to learn coding or basic graphic design? It may be true that leaving your relationship tomorrow would put you in a financial pickle. But that doesn't mean you can't start *planning* for your future today. Not being highly employable is a state that can be changed. And the sooner you start, the faster you'll be able to leave your unsatisfying relationship and get on with your life.

One excuse I hear from my clients all the time is that they want to quit their job and start their own business—but they don't know how they'll pay the rent in the meantime. So what are the facts? They don't have enough savings to quit their job tomorrow. Okay—that's logical. But it turns into an excuse when they use their lack of savings as a reason to stay in a job they deplore for months on end, without ever taking any action to improve things. What about starting a business on the side, building it in their free time?

Often, the response I get to that question is another excuse: They have no free time. In this case, I use the facts in our favor. I take them through an inventory of how they're spending their time. Looking at it on the page, they realize they *could* carve out a couple of hours a week to build a website or take an online training course. I did my coaching certification while I was still a full-time employee at Hay House. I can attest that one or two hours a week soon adds up to a lot of knowledge and skill!

Here are some other excuse-busting possibilities:

- Taking out a loan

- Asking for funding from a friend, mentor, or loved one

- Getting a scholarship or grant

- Educating yourself online

- Finding a friend to teach you skills in exchange for something you can offer besides money

- Taking just one or two classes at a time

- Offering to do some work as an intern to gain experience

- Starting your own business doing something you already know how to do

- Brainstorming with friends to find resources or skills you didn't know you had (like we did in Step Two)

The *truth* is that we're living in a time that's ripe for entrepreneurs. More people are making money in creative and unconventional ways than perhaps ever before.

When you can separate fact from fiction, fact from belief, and truth from excuse, you can finally let go of those excuses and take real action toward financial ease—or whatever it is you desire!

EXERCISE #11: TAKE STOCK OF YOUR EXCUSES

1. Look back at the beliefs you wrote down in Exercises #7 and #8 in Step Three. Now that you've had practice determining one of your excuses in Exercise #10,

write down the excuse related to each of your top five beliefs. Try the "I can't" approach, but if that doesn't work, don't worry. If your belief and your excuse sound exactly the same, that's fine. Here's an example using "I can't":

Belief: "I will always struggle."

Excuse: "I can't get a better a job or take a course or improve my circumstances because I will always struggle."

Rephrased excuse: "I'm *resistant to* getting a better job or taking a course or improving my circumstances because I *believe* I will always struggle."

Now, write yours down.

2. Next, look at your belief/excuse combo, and ask yourself: If this belief and excuse disappeared tomorrow, what could/would I do in my life that I can't do now? Write down what comes to mind without censoring. For example, "If I didn't believe I will always struggle, I could go beyond getting a better job. I could start my own business!"

3. Do you feel excited about the possibilities? Can you see yourself letting go of the belief and excuse, or does it feel like it will take you a while? If it still doesn't feel possible, don't worry. As you continue through the steps, you'll get closer and closer, I promise!

You Can't Afford Not to Drop the Excuses

There are huge costs to not dropping our excuses, as Whitney's story proves. She was a live-beyond-your-means kind of gal, who told herself she needed to have the best of everything even though she couldn't afford it. But then she'd whip out the "I can't afford it" excuse when it came to the more mundane expenses. Like, say, homeowner's insurance. (Can you tell where this is going?)

One night, Whitney accidentally left a candle burning. Her house *burned down.*

Believe it or not, the story gets even worse—because Whitney was so distrusting of banks that she had all of her savings in an envelope in a drawer.

In the house. That burned down.

Her overspending—and the excuses it generated—literally cost her everything except the cash in her pocket and the shirt on her back. She was so humiliated by the experience that she used her last $10 to buy a pair of cheap sunglasses—so she could avoid looking anyone in the eye.

Okay, maybe that's an extreme example. But excuses cost us in small ways, every day. As you've seen in the stories you've already read, they keep us in debt, prevent us from making as much money as we could, and block us from taking advantage of opportunities that are all around us. In my case, that opportunity was the 401(k) plan offered by Hay House. In the 12 years I worked there, I never took advantage of their savings matching plan. My excuse was that I didn't understand it (the classic "I don't know how" excuse), and I had no one to ask. Really? Hello, there were dozens of people working around me at the company, all of whom had figured it out and could explain it to me. When I look back, I realize I didn't ask because I didn't want to appear stupid. Feeling stupid triggered my worthiness issues, and I didn't want to go there. In the process, I lost a lot of free money.

My excuses also cost me in terms of vacation time. When you're working for a company that offers you vacation, those paid days off are basically free money, too. I didn't take any vacation for 12 years because of my belief that I had to work all the time and be indispensable in order to be worthy. I had all kinds of excuses for not taking vacation: "They need me"; "No one can do the job without me." None of which proved to be true!

How many weeks of free time—and free money—did I throw away over those 12 years? A lot! And all because of my belief that I wasn't worthy, and the excuses I made up to support it.

The emotional costs of our excuses are also great. The high price tag includes our self-worth, self-trust, self-respect, and integrity. It includes depression, staying in unsatisfying relationships, and living in fear of never fulfilling our dreams. What are *your* excuses costing you?

Death to Excuses!

Debbie Ford suggested that we make our lives an "excuse-free zone." Can you make that declaration and stick to it? Now, I know that excuses are habits, so you might find yourself falling back into one or two unconsciously. The idea isn't to be perfect, but to commit to staying as aware of your excuses as you can—while finding creative ways to overcome them. This doesn't mean you have to run off and do something extreme like quit your job or get a divorce. But awareness will help you see obstacles as problems to be solved, rather than brick walls!

Embracing Risk

So many of our excuses are based on what we experienced in the past. Maybe we had a failure at some point, so we want to avoid that kind of hurt ever again. Hey, I get it! Nobody wants to get hurt. But we can't live in a plastic bubble either. Living a great life requires some risk.

The truth is it makes no sense to live your life today based on what happened in the past. You aren't the same person you were even a month ago, let alone years ago, so why live as though you can't do more now than you did before? Obviously, you're game to work on yourself—if you weren't, you wouldn't be reading this book right now. Just by virtue of your willingness, there's greater possibility available to you now than you've ever had before.

Sure, making any big change takes courage. But that's usually *all* it takes. Think about me and all that money I had stockpiled. If it weren't for my financial advisor, I would never have thought to pay off my mortgage and ultimately save myself thousands of dollars in financing costs. Where was the risk *really*? It wasn't where I thought it was. The greater risk was in holding on to the funds out of fear and not getting the information I needed to make a wiser choice. The best choice didn't take nearly as much courage as I feared it would. Have you ever been afraid of something, then found out your fears were pretty much unfounded? Yeah—me, too. Lots of times.

I always try to remember not to beat myself up for excuses that held me back in the past. We can't turn back the clock, but we can start again right now. Your choices today will predict your future.

The bottom line is this: What's more of a priority for you—feeling safe, or living the greatest life you could possibly live? If that question brings up anxiety for you, I understand.

It used to freak me out completely. The key is to breathe, and just notice the anxiety. Reassure your child self that you're not in any literal danger. Remember that the risks of staying in a tight, protective life are great, too. In fact, those risks are often even greater than the ones we fear the most. They say people at the end of life don't so much regret what they did as what they *didn't* do.

This quote has been used a lot, but that's because it really says it best:

> *"And the day came when the risk to remain tight in a bud was more painful than the risk it took to blossom."*
>
> *– attributed to Anaïs Nin*

If you think about it, mustering courage is not such a terrible obstacle. You just need to work on developing it within yourself. After all, if you never try, you're defeated before you even start. So the excuses *themselves* are the real obstacles we must overcome in order to live the lives we were meant to live.

A big part of developing more courage in yourself is increasing your self-worth. The more worthy you feel, the more courageous you'll feel. It really does work that way. How? If your worth isn't tied to your success or failure, what do you have to lose? You *know* you're still worthy even if something doesn't work out exactly right the first time or if somebody else judges you. It's a beautiful thing!

EXERCISE #12: FROM EXCUSES TO ACTION

This is a weeklong exercise to help you begin to notice more of your excuses. Then, you can choose actions to break the excuse cycle and begin to get unstuck from the habit of "I can't."

1. For a week, pay attention to your excuses. Every time you hear yourself using one (aloud or silently), write it down.

2. At the end of the week, look at the excuses you recorded. For each one, see if you can determine the corresponding belief. (Remember that sometimes your excuses and beliefs will be identical. That's fine!)

3. Now, for each belief and excuse combo, write down the new belief (like you did in Exercise #9 in Step Three). This new belief will help you break free from the excuse.

4. Next, if it isn't already clear, write down what each excuse is preventing you from doing. What do you want to do that your excuse says you "can't" do?

5. Lastly, write down one action that you can take to begin to let go of the excuse and do what you really want to do. Make it one small action—something that feels doable and isn't too drastic.

    Here's an example:

    Belief: "I could never make it on my own."

    Excuse: "I can't leave my unhappy marriage because I'd never make it on my own."

    What my excuse prevents me from doing: "My excuse is preventing me from leaving my marriage and starting the new life I want."

    New belief: "I have many skills and talents that I could use to make it on my own."

Potential Actions: "I'll knit scarves and sell them on Etsy."

Or "I'll take an online course in website design."

Or "I'll help a friend clean up her clutter and ask her to refer me to her friends, who can become paying clients."

Affirm Your Worth

"I'm worthy of taking action toward a better future that brings me wealth in every area of my life."

UNCOVER YOUR UNDERLYING COMMITMENTS

When I first met Abby, she was trying to break free from living paycheck to paycheck. Her excuse up until that point was that she was already getting paid better than her peers at her company, so more money wasn't available. Through our work together on this process, she unearthed a shadow belief about rich people. "The wealthy are greedy and dishonest," she said. She traced that belief back to statements she heard her parents say when she was a kid.

Uncovering that belief was quite a shocker for Abby! Even after bringing the belief to light and becoming aware of the excuses she had made to uphold that belief, Abby felt stuck. It was a belief that had taken hold when she was probably five or six years old—so young that she unconsciously felt it was fact. She could see that it was just a misinformed belief, yet she was at a loss as to how to disengage from it.

Then there's Kim, who's been living with a pattern that's become a vicious circle. She's struggling financially, and as a result, she feels she can't have the relationship she really wants. "My belief is that I'm not worthy to meet the man of my dreams while I'm in this financial state. I tell myself that I need to get my act together, have all my debt paid off, and be running a successful business before I can attract 'the one.'" Her excuse is "I can't have a relationship because I'm 'financially unattractive.'"

Kim really wants a relationship, and she really wants to create the financial ease that would make her feel "financially attractive" enough for a partner. But she keeps making excuses for not paying off her debts or starting her new business. Why? She's figured out her beliefs and her excuses. What else could be in the way?

Abby and Kim have fallen prey to a phenomenon that we've all experienced—except most of us don't know it. That's why this step is called *Uncover Your Underlying Commitments.*

What's an Underlying Commitment?

"Underlying commitment" is a term Debbie Ford created. Others have called them "unconscious commitments" or "hidden commitments." They're commitments we made to ourselves when we were very young as a result of the limiting beliefs we developed. We don't know about them because they're in the shadows of the unconscious, underlying our conscious knowledge.

When we get stuck in a pattern that we can't seem to change no matter how hard we try, it's almost certainly the result of an underlying commitment. We think we're committed to one thing, but we're actually committed to something else. For example, let's say you think you're committed to starting your own business. But your underlying commitment is actually to stay safe and small right where you are. Even as you make efforts to start your own business, some part of you is sabotaging those efforts and ensuring you fail.

Underlying commitments cause us to take actions that lead us *away from* the direction of our dreams. To get stuck in patterns that we can't seem to change no matter how hard we try. To create results that are inconsistent with what we say we desire. But the truth is that we're always getting what we're *actually* committed to—our underlying, hidden commitments.

Let's explore our example in more detail: Say you want to start your own business, but you grew up in a family that always struggled financially. So at a young age, you formed the belief that in order to fit into your family—and thus, stay safe—you would need to struggle with money as well. Because of that belief, you made a promise to yourself that you would avoid your finances in order to avoid pain. In fact, you spent years doing just that. You've been to seminars; you've practiced manifesting meditations; you've written abundance affirmations. You've even worked on discovering your limiting beliefs and your excuses. Maybe you've even gone so far as to finally start that business . . . only to have it crash and burn. What's going on?

Because you formed the belief that you'll always struggle with money—and promised yourself that you'd avoid your finances—you're creating a reality characterized by struggle. You're actually *committed* to struggle and avoidance. Now, why would anyone stay committed to such a thing when it comes at such a high cost? Because to the little girl inside, it feels safe. Remember, this commitment is unconscious and began when you were very young.

At the young age that our commitments were formed, they felt vital for our survival. They may not make sense to us as adults, but that doesn't matter. They still have a hold deep down in our psyches.

In this situation, your inner child is accustomed to struggling with money. It's what she knew growing up, so it's comfortable. In her little mind, it's the best! She doesn't have to take the risk of owning a business or even learning how to live as someone with more money. She doesn't have to stretch her self-worth to accommodate the kind of empowerment that greater wealth would bring. To that young girl inside, the underlying commitment to avoid her finances has a whole host of great benefits. To the adult you, though, that underlying commitment could be the bane of your existence.

Can you see the secret in all of this? *We are always creating exactly the reality we're most committed to having.* It doesn't matter what we *say* we want. If we don't have the thing we desire, it's because we're *more* committed to our present state than we are to getting what we want. I know—yuck! I felt the same way when I first got this.

But I also felt how true it was. My hidden commitments were the main obstacles that stood between what I said I wanted and what I actually had. For example, I always said I wanted a powerful, self-sufficient man with a steady income. But what I got was someone who was dependent on me financially. My underlying commitment was to make sure I was loved, through "earning" my worth. That was based on my belief that I wasn't worthy if I didn't take care of everyone else's needs. It became an excuse to stay in the marriage. I said I wanted to be loved for who I was, but secretly, I didn't believe it was possible. I believed that if I left, I would fail— which would make me feel even more unworthy. So I was unconsciously committed to having just what I had and staying right where I was.

Our underlying commitments are our *first* and *strongest* commitments because they were formed when we were so young and vulnerable and impressionable. As a result, the belief that I had to earn my worth was so strong that it kept me stuck in an unsatisfying marriage—not to mention tied to the commitment that I would never be loved for who I am.

All of this, of course, was unconscious . . . until I did the work to bring it to light. Once I brought it into my conscious awareness, I could take the action to disengage from the beliefs, excuses, and underlying commitments I had formed. You've already worked on ways to create new beliefs, and you've begun to disengage from your resulting excuses. In this chapter, you'll work on bringing your underlying commitments out of the shadows and begin to affirm your commitment to what you *really* want.

As you continue to work through the steps, you'll strengthen that resolve by increasing your self-worth. (That's our very next step! Are you excited?) Again, the more worthy we feel, the less inclined we are to stay tied to beliefs, excuses, and underlying commitments that prevent us from having the life we *know* we deserve.

What Do Underlying Commitments Sound Like?

To help you figure out your own underlying commitments, let's look at what they often sound like compared to what we *think* we're committed to.

"I *think* I'm committed to becoming a public speaker."

Underlying commitment: "I'm committed to staying small so that I won't be called stupid."

"I *think* I want to start my own business."

Underlying commitment: "I'm committed to controlling everything so I feel safe, and having my own business feels very out of control."

"I *think* I'm committed to becoming an artist."

Underlying commitment: "I'm committed to being an accountant because that's what my father was, and he died when I was young. I'll dishonor him if I do something else."

As you can see, your desire and your underlying commitment may not be directly related to one another!

EXERCISE #13: WHERE ARE YOUR COMMITMENTS HIDING?

How do you begin to figure out what underlying uncon- scious commitments you hold? One way is to look at your life and examine your decisions, actions, patterns of behavior, and habitual choices. This exercise will guide you in asking yourself important questions that can make you more aware of your unconscious motivations.

1. Write down a desire you have in your life that hasn't come to fruition despite your best efforts.

2. Now, remember the teaching on underlying commit- ments. Even though you aren't getting what you want, what you have in this area of your life is in perfect alignment with what you've been most committed to in your unconscious. Considering this truth, what do you think your underlying commitment is? Write what some possible unconscious commitments might be. For example, "I desire financial ease." My underlying commitment might be "I'm committed to staying in debt because I don't feel worthy of having money." Or "I'm committed to having little money because pover- ty is in my comfort zone from childhood." Don't worry if you're unable to get to what you think is the core

underlying commitment right away. You can continue to explore potential underlying commitments related to this and other desires.

3. Think about choices and behaviors that have been driven by your underlying commitment. Write them down. For example, "I've bought things I didn't really need, and that's kept me in debt." "I passed on an opportunity for a new job because I was afraid, but I told myself it wasn't the right job for me."

4. If you struggled to unearth your underlying commitments, imagine that you're thinking of someone else. What might someone with your behaviors, or who made your choices, be unconsciously committed to? Write down any ideas that come to mind.

5. Next, take one of your underlying commitments, and think about when you may have formed it. You were probably under the age of ten. What situation or environment may have led you to make this promise to yourself? Write down what you remember.

6. Write down a new conscious commitment to replace the old unconscious underlying commitment you discovered. What do you really want to be committed to?

7. Write down one new action you can take that will help you move toward your conscious commitment. If this feels too frightening, that's okay. Then see if you can choose a small action. Maybe it will be as simple as doing something nice for yourself this week that will boost your self-worth.

The Circle of Beliefs-Commitments-Excuses

Alicia's first money memory is walking into a grand, colonial-style bank building with her mother to open a savings account when she was five years old. "It always felt special, like someplace I'd dress up to go," she says. But the experience also created a belief that money is for saving, not spending. Out of that belief came the commitment "I promise not to spend money on myself." She could use all sorts of excuses to uphold that commitment, including "I can't spend money on myself because it's more blessed to give than to receive."

Like with Alicia, a vicious circle of beliefs, commitments, and excuses often gets in the way of our desires. Take the utterly nonfinancial desire to lose weight. (Which most of us have toyed with once or twice in our lifetimes!) Say you have the belief that if you put yourself out into the dating pool, you're likely to get rejected . . . or hurt. The corresponding excuse might be "I can't date because I'm too fat." While you might talk about wanting to lose weight, and maybe even go on a diet, the underlying commitment is to stay over-weight in the (hidden) hope that nobody will ask you out. This commitment will show up as *lack* of commitment to losing weight. "I'll eat these cookies tonight, and I'll go on my diet tomorrow," or "A little bit of ice cream never hurt anybody." As always, until the work has been done to dis-engage it, the underlying commitment—in this case, to stay plump—will win out.

Let's look at it this way: Our shadow beliefs are what we came to accept as facts when we were children. Our excuses and underlying commitments are our strategy for enforcing those beliefs that we think of as hard truths. Here's an example:

Shadow belief: "You need a college education in order to amount to anything in this world."

Excuse: "There's no reason for me to apply for a better job—they'd never hire me without a degree."

Underlying commitment: "I'm committed to staying safe in my place so that no one can say, 'Who does she think she is? She's not good enough for that job!'"

Another story I hear frequently has to do with accomplishing big things in life. Many of us feel like we're destined for greatness, but our beliefs keep us from really going for it. For example, we might think that if we "go big" in our lives, everything will spin out of control. Like Chloe in the last chapter, we think we'll be too busy to have downtime. Or we won't have time to find love or enjoy simple pleasures. This belief programs a commitment to staying small, which is held in place by excuses: "I'd love to try and become a life coach, but I can't because I'm too busy to take the training." "I can't afford it—maybe next year."

The circle of beliefs, commitments, and excuses isn't always easy to penetrate. But let's try to unearth some more of your commitments by looking at how these three interact.

EXERCISE #14: THE VICIOUS CIRCLE

Let's not only see how this circle of beliefs–commitments–excuses operates in your psyche but how you can begin to reprogram yourself by choosing new beliefs and commitments. (No need to replace the excuses!)

1. List three different desires that you haven't yet been able to create in your life.

2.   Go back through your beliefs and excuses from Exercises #7, #8, #10, #11, and #12 in Steps Three and Four, as well as the underlying commitments you wrote down in Exercise #13 from this chapter. For each of your desires, see if you can identify the belief, excuse, and/or underlying commitment that's keeping you from getting what you want.

Here's an example:

Desire: "I want to earn more money."

Underlying commitment: "I'm committed to staying in debt."

Limiting belief: "I'm not the kind of person who can get a great job or start my own business."

Excuse: "I can't try for a new job or start my own business because I'll fail."

3.   Now, ask yourself what you would have to give up if you made a new commitment. In our example, the answer might be "My fear of failure."

4.   Finally, write down a new belief and a new commitment to replace the ones you don't want. Here are examples:

New belief: "I'm capable of doing anything I set my mind to."

New commitment: "I'm committed to paying off my debt little by little so that I can make my dream come true."

Success Stories

Underlying commitments can be tenacious, but take heart. Just bringing them into awareness is often enough to begin to disengage them. Here are some success stories to give you more confidence.

Sheila had an underlying commitment that had kept her stuck in limiting patterns—and stuck in a job she hated. "What's really bad is feeling chained to work, and a slave to an income level that doesn't allow me to express all of myself in the world," she says.

More than anything, she wanted to create financial ease, and she tried all kinds of techniques. But nothing panned out. Then, in our work together with this process, she discovered a shadow belief that "people want to take everything from me." This is a belief that she learned from her parents early on, and it has stuck to her like glue. To avoid being "taken," she's stayed unconsciously committed to having "just enough"—so that she has little for anyone to take. "I penny-pinch and guard every single dollar. I waste precious time and energy doing so," she admits. "Even though I consciously desire full financial freedom, I've been more committed to not being 'had.' As a result, I've created no excess or abundance that I can be tricked out of. This has kept me trapped inside my own life. What I'm realizing now is that it wouldn't actually be the end of the world to be tricked out of some of my money, as long as I felt free to create more abundance and learn from those experiences."

Then, there's Crystal. She tried everything to get herself to keep a clean house. She took courses in how to clean properly. She set schedules for herself. She tried every imaginable discipline, but her house was always a mess. She hated it, but nothing seemed to work. When Crystal's mother came over, she looked at her daughter's house and shook her head. This left Crystal feeling ashamed.

Finally, Crystal discovered that she had a limiting belief that "cleaning is drudgery." And she had all kinds of excuses to uphold that belief. "I'm too tired." "I'll clean tomorrow." "If I make up the bed now, it's just going to be unmade again in the morning." When Crystal began to think more about her childhood, she realized that her mother was a neat freak. "My mother always made me dust, and I was allergic to dust mites. I'd start to feel sick, but I didn't even know why. Now, I take allergy shots, so I *can* dust. But the truth is that my underlying commitment is to *not* be a clean freak like my mom. No, I want to be a free spirit!" In this case, Crystal's underlying commitment was to rebel against what she disliked in her childhood!

Now that Crystal knows about this, she can begin to disengage from it, realizing that cleaning doesn't have to prevent her from being a free spirit. Plus, she doesn't have to become a "clean freak" like her mom if she doesn't want to.

Beth has a dream of becoming a successful writer and performer. She says that's what she wants, but she never seems to get it. Why? Well, she's lived her entire life with the belief that hard work can kill you. "I came from a family of workaholics who became alcoholics and addicts, and they worked themselves to the bone," she says. The situation even led one of her family members to commit suicide. Her fearful belief has been that she would do the same, becoming consumed by work and losing control of her life to the point that it would actually kill her.

As a result, when opportunities come her way, she often runs in the other direction. She's good at coming up with excuses for why she runs. "I can't because my kids need me too much." "I don't know how to do that anyway." She has the unconscious commitment to never work too hard. That commitment comes out of the deep-seated fear that developed when she was very young.

Happily, she's becoming conscious of this underlying commitment. Even though she still feels the fear, she's taking steps toward the life she wants. "Whenever I start to feel scared, I remind myself that I'm in control. I know I won't allow myself to be consumed by work. I can go for what I want and make choices that will keep me from working too hard."

And remember Abby from the top of the chapter? She had the belief that "wealthy people are greedy and dishonest." So her underlying commitment was to never, ever become one of them! Once she started to see how her unconscious commitment had kept her impoverished, she mustered up the courage to walk into her boss's office—and ask for a raise.

Underlying Commitments as Identity

Sometimes, we identify with our underlying commitments to such a degree that they become a big part of who we believe we are. In order to let go of them, we might have to give up an identity we've carried our whole life—as someone who isn't smart or worthy enough, perhaps. We might have to defy the voice of a parent, who told us we'd never be successful. We might have to surpass our family's circumstances—even if it makes them uncomfortable that we have money while they continue to struggle.

In this case, it takes special courage to risk going for what we really want. If you feel that the underlying commitments you discover are a part of your identity, stay aware that you may need to keep reminding yourself of who you *want* to be, not who you've always been.

Digging Deeper

Yes, it's true that some underlying commitments can be more easily unearthed than others. And some of them can be disengaged quickly, while others take a lot of time and work. If you find that you have some difficult underlying commitments in there, you're far from alone. Most of us have some big ones. Just keep digging. This is the work we have to do as human beings! The unconscious is filled with information for us to bring into awareness and our lives get better and better the further we go.

Let's look at some examples of clients who are still working to get to the core underlying commitment that's standing in their way. Remember Kim's story from early in the chapter? Her self-worth is very much entangled with money. That's why she feels she isn't worthy of a relationship until she has her financial "ducks in a row." If she digs deeper, though, she might discover even more limiting beliefs, excuses, and underlying commitments. She might find out that she's so afraid of being hurt in a relationship that she stays committed to her suppressed financial situation. Her belief that she can't have a relationship until she's "financially attractive" may be protecting her inner child from the inherent risk of falling in love.

Noele has recently come to terms with her underlying commitment to stay miserable. Why would anyone have a commitment to such a thing? Noele isn't exactly sure, but it probably originated in childhood. Little kids just want to belong. If a child sees unhappy people all around her, she might feel it's safer to feel bad. Playing the role of the unhappy victim can also have its benefits. It can make us feel special and elicit pity from others. This might be the only way we know how to get love when we're young.

Dawn's dream is to start her own business. But no matter what she does, she can't seem to make it happen. She and her family always seem to be struggling financially, so she's constantly trying to make ends meet. She's buried so deep under her financial obligations that she can't imagine leaving her job and becoming an entrepreneur. "The majority of our money goes to paying off our debt. Therefore, everything else is secondary. It keeps me stuck in the same old pattern of 'not having enough.' We've paid off credit cards several times and always manage to build up debt again. Having that debt prevents me from jumping into building my own business. It keeps me stuck in a job I don't really love," she says.

Clearly, Dawn is committed to *not* starting her own business. We would have to dig a little deeper to discover where this commitment comes from, but it probably comes back to a fear of failure. She needs to pinpoint when this fear of failure took hold in her young psyche, and why. She might be able to unearth her commitment by asking herself about her "what ifs." What if she loses all her money? What if she discovers she's not good enough? As far as her inner child is concerned, it's better to just stay where she is . . . and blame her debt.

Since underlying commitments are often difficult to unearth, it can be helpful to get a reflection from someone you trust. You might want to work with a therapist, coach, or trusted friend to help you bring your commitments to the surface. What's more, most of us actually have *layers* of commitments. We discover one, only to find an even deeper one hiding underneath. Usually, when we unearth one that's really potent, we have an "aha!" moment or start to feel emotional. That's when we know we're onto something!

Remember, if you find yourself getting stuck, don't worry. You're making progress! I find that part of my life is always about self-discovery. The more I learn about myself, the more my self-worth increases—and the more easily I can make better, more conscious choices for my life. Allow the process to unfold and be patient. Every step forward is a positive one.

By exposing your unconscious commitments, you're gaining the ability to see and tell yourself the truth. You can step into a greater sense of worthiness—one that says, "I feel compassion for my child self's beliefs and commitments, but it's time for me as an adult to commit to what I truly deserve."

EXERCISE #15: OPEN YOUR HEART

This exercise is designed to help you understand that your underlying commitments were put into place to protect you. It will also help you identify any fears about living by a new commitment. The child within is almost bound to feel afraid of that kind of change. If you open your heart with compassion, it will be easier to begin to switch to a more conscious commitment.

1. Choose one of the underlying commitments you discovered in Exercise #13 or #14.

2. How has this commitment served or benefited you in the past? In what ways has it kept you safe? Write down your thoughts.

3. Now, open your heart and feel compassion for the child you were. That child probably felt threatened and scared. Can you thank your inner child self for making this commitment to keeping you safe, even though it isn't working for you anymore? Can you make peace with the commitment, knowing that it was put in place to serve and protect you?

4. Honor the gifts of the commitment. Notice how you've always had the power, creativity, and ability to get what you've been most committed to.

5. Now, gently let the child in you know that you don't need this commitment to stay safe any longer. Affirm that you will no longer allow this commitment to have a stronghold over your life. Make note of any anxiety that comes up as you make that affirmation.

6. Close your eyes, and take several minutes to imagine what your life would be like if you were devoted to your new commitment rather than the old one. Notice if your mind starts wandering to all the reasons this new commitment will never work out. If it does, simply come back to imagining your life with this new commitment in place.

7. Did any fears come up about living based on your new conscious commitment? If so, write them down.

8. Review the fears you wrote down. Do any of them give you new insights about other beliefs, excuses, and underlying commitments that are holding you back? If so, write those down as well.

9. What new structure can you put into place to support you in giving up the old nonserving underlying commitment? What new conscious commitment can you insert into your awareness to serve you in the fulfillment of your desire? What would you need to make this new commitment part of your personal operating system from now on? Write down any ideas that come to mind.

10. If you aren't yet sure what to do to put your new commitment into action, take heart. It will become clearer as you continue working through the steps in this book.

The work you're doing will help increase your feelings of worthiness. The more worthy you feel, the more you'll be able to see the next right step.

Affirm Your Worth

"I'm committed to the bright future I know I deserve."

BECOME WILLING TO BE WORTHY

I was the Event Director at Hay House for 12 years. It was a dream job in so many ways, and I loved it. I was the one behind the scenes putting everyone else out into the light, and I was good at it. But in time, I longed to be in the light myself. I began craving the opportunity to use more of my gifts and my own personal experience in another capacity to help others. I wanted to be a coach, an author, a speaker.

There was one problem: I had long been tied to the belief that I had to be "Superwoman" in order to "earn" my worth. If I were working for myself, how worthy could I possibly be? Would my beloved friends in the Hay House family still love me if I no longer performed for them as I had done for so many years? Not to mention all the "what ifs" that came into my head—"What if I fall flat on my face?" "What if I end up without a job *or* a career?"

Buoyed by my underlying commitment to be indispensable, I developed excuses to stay in the job, and thus stay safe. "I can't make a living 'only' as an author, speaker, and coach," I told myself. My beliefs, excuses, and commitments were holding me back.

It took me some time to understand that I'm not loved for what I *do*. I'm truly loved—by both my family of friends at

WORTHY

Hay House and the people I know outside of work—for who
I *am*. To them, my worth is unconditional.

Reid Tracy, the president and CEO of Hay House, has
always been my greatest cheerleader and most trusted advisor. So when I finally told him I wanted to quit my job and he
said, "I'll tell you when it's time to quit," I listened. He urged
me to wait just a bit longer. "Stay here a little while and use
the time to build your platform," he advised. "Then you'll
have a firm foundation under you when you leave."

He was right. By "platform," Reid meant making myself
more known in the world by pursuing a "side hustle"—
building my coaching practice, publishing my book, getting
some speaking engagements, and writing magazine articles. Then, my practice would be solid enough that I would
be able to make it without the full-time job.

I spent over a year doing that work while still working at
Hay House, and I loved it. Clearly, my "side job" was what I
was meant to do. During that year, I also worked on my self-
worth. It was only by becoming *willing to be worthy* of the life
I wanted that I was able to finally leave Hay House and go out
into the world, on my own as *me*—full-time.

In the interest of full disclosure, Reid had to give me a
little push. "It's time for you to go out on your own," he said
one day on the phone. This came not long after he delivered
the huge news to me that Hay House wanted to pick up my
self-published book, *Jump . . . And Your Life Will Appear,* and
publish it as a full-fledged Hay House title! My fears were still
a bit in my way, even after I had created a strong enough
platform for myself. In fact, the first thing I said to him was,
"You're firing me?!" And then I burst into tears on the phone.
He said, "What are you talking about? This was our plan
all along!"

Thankfully, my sense of worthiness was strong enough by then to ultimately say "yes" to my new life. I took a deep breath and made the jump. But what does "strong enough" self-worth look like? Well, that's what Step Six is all about: *Become Willing to Be Worthy.* This is where we get to the core of the process.

We'll explore what it's like to feel worthy, what it's like to *not* feel worthy, and more about where those feelings of unworthiness come from. Then, we'll do exercises that begin to expand your sense of worthiness *right now.*

The Picture of Worthiness

How do we take stock of our worthiness quotient? First and foremost, we start to notice when we're judging ourselves. One of the easiest ways to tell if your self-worth could use a tune-up is by paying attention to how you judge yourself. Do you get very upset when you make a mistake? Do you say, "Damn! I'm such an idiot!" Do you tell yourself that you aren't smart enough, aren't good enough, aren't capable?

Sometimes, that voice of judgment is so automatic that we don't actually "hear" it, but we sure do feel it. The excuses come next. "Oh, I can't join that class. It's stupid." "I can't take that job. It's too far away. What a commute that would be!" Underneath those excuses is the longing for the very thing we're pushing away. And we push it away because we're afraid we aren't good enough.

Also underneath the excuses are our "what ifs"—"What if I'm not good enough to get that job?" "What if I'm not smart enough to keep up in that class?" We would rather stay safe and small than take the risk of finding out that our "what ifs" are correct.

But here's the thing: When your self-worth is strong, the "what ifs" aren't so scary. *What if* you take the class and find out you can't keep up? So what? If your self-worth is solid, it won't be damaged. You aren't going to die if you can't keep up in some class! The same is true of that job. If you don't get it, so what? It's hardly the only job in the world. With a strong sense of worthiness, we're much less likely to let "failures" get us down. Instead, we see them as learning experiences that propel us forward to even *better* opportunities.

Frequently, our "what ifs" are tied to what others will think about us. Let's take public speaking as an example. Surveys show that next to death, speaking in front of large groups is most people's worst nightmare. But why? Because they're afraid they'll be ridiculed. Once again, we put our self-worth in the hands of other people. But if someone is going to stop loving us because we aren't able to give a good speech, what is that person's value system? If you really stop to think about it, what kind of person would stop loving you for a reason like that?

Then there are our own self-judgments—the inner voice that says we're not doing it (whatever "it" is) well enough. That we haven't earned our worth because we haven't performed well enough. When others judge us, they hold up a mirror to our worst judgments of ourselves. That's why gaining self-worth is an inside job!

The condition of our self-worth is also revealed in how well we care for ourselves. Just as we demonstrate our love for others through our actions, we demonstrate self-worth through making sure we're eating well, sleeping enough, and exercising enough. We nurture ourselves, taking time for what we need in order to feel good. That might be meditation. A walk in the park. A hot bath. A talk with a friend. Alone time.

It also means taking credit for our progress and our successes. We pat ourselves on the back when we do something well. We acknowledge our talents and abilities. We notice our growth.

Healthy pride comes from a place of knowing your worth. Arrogance actually comes from a *lack* of self-worth. It's putting on a good show of self-worth, but it isn't *real* worthiness. Do you know someone who has healthy self-confidence, yet isn't boastful or arrogant? That person could be a good role model. Even if you don't know anyone personally, you can probably find someone in public life who exhibits that kind of confidence. What would it feel like to take healthy pride in what you do and who you are?

Remember there's no "ultimate" or "perfect" state of self-worth. No matter where you start, you have the opportunity to improve. So let's look at ways you can increase your willingness to be worthy.

EXERCISE #16: CHECK THE STATE OF YOUR SELF-WORTH

In what areas do you need to work on your self-worth? Let's take a look and prescribe some antidotes to help boost your worth before we go any further. This exercise has three parts.

Part 1: *Judgments*

1. Let's explore judgments you hold about yourself. This first part may not be fun, but it's worth it. Write down the five to ten top things that get you down in your life—the things you blame yourself for the most. Think

of so-called "failures," or moments you felt really hurt, ashamed, embarrassed, or sad. Here are some examples:

"I failed first grade."

"I yelled at my mother."

"My dad told me I was selfish."

"I haven't been able to sustain a relationship for more than a year."

"No matter what I do, I can't seem to get a promotion."

2. Next, write down what you've made each of these incidents mean about your worth. For example, "I failed first grade" could have made you believe "I'm stupid." "I haven't been able to sustain a relationship for more than a year" could have made you believe "I'm unlovable."

3. Now, write down at least three reasons why the judgment/belief you developed as a result of each incident is not true. Here are some possible reasons for our example:

"I'm stupid because I failed first grade."

"This isn't true because I went on to be on the honor roll in high school."

"This isn't true because I've successfully gotten and sustained a number of good jobs."

"This isn't true because I have a great talent for helping others feel better about themselves."

Part 2: *Self-Care*

4. On a scale from 1 to 5—with 5 meaning you're doing great and 1 meaning you're not doing well at all—rate how well you're caring for yourself in these areas:

Diet __

Exercise __

Sleep __

Quiet Time/Meditation/Alone Time __

5. For any area in which you scored yourself 1, 2, or 3, write down one action you can take right away to take better care of yourself. For example, "I'll look online for ways I can improve the quality of my sleep and try one of them tonight." Every self-loving action you take today will immediately boost your self-worth and make you want to do more.

Part 3: *Celebrate Your Successes*

6. Make a list of five to ten successes you've experienced in the last few years. Include professional, personal, and self-growth experiences. For example, you might say:

"I took a photography class."

"I stopped losing my temper with my children as much."

"I gained several new friends in a supportive community."

"My friend's toddler told me he loves me."

"I won an award at work."

7. Now, read those successes over again, and bask in them. You've done all that! Don't you feel more worthy already?

Whose Voice Are You Listening to?

In the last exercise, you explored some of the judgments you have about yourself, many of which probably stem from old childhood beliefs. Some of our self-judgments are based on misinterpreting what someone else says, or presuming we know what they're thinking about us. We conclude that they're judging us, and that judgment becomes a belief in our own psyche. But the truth is that the other person may not be judging us at all. He or she might just be angry in the moment due to lack of sleep or an upset stomach. The comment or action might have nothing to do with us, but we make it mean something about our worth.

Think about how often we assume someone else is judging us. We do it a lot as adults. But when we were kids, we did it times *a hundred*. At a young age, we only know who we are in reference to other people. We form our self-identity based on what others—parents, siblings, relatives, teachers, friends at school—reflect back to us. We assume the grown-ups around us know what they're talking about. If an adult says there is something wrong with us, it must be true. Heck, even if some kid we dislike, who sits next to us in class, says, "Something's wrong with you," we usually believe it's the truth.

Only it isn't.

Now that you're an adult, you know that we all say things at times out of nothing more than our own frustration. Often, we don't mean what we say in those moments. We don't think that other people are taking our opinions so much to heart. Most parents don't realize their kids are taking offhand comments like "What's wrong with you?" as gospel.

But as we grow up, these voices of our parents, as well as others in our lives, become our own. We repeat in our heads the same words we heard. Like our beliefs about money or anything else, we then relate to those words as fact.

Lizzie says a belief she got from her sister's voice has been "running her life forever." When Lizzie was somewhere between the ages of four and six years old, her sister repeatedly told her that nobody would love her because she had curly red hair and was therefore different. She's now coming to terms with the fact that her shadow belief that nobody will ever love her is merely based on her sister's voice. And that it's untrue.

Sometimes, it isn't words—it's the *behavior* of the adults or others around us that we interpret as meaning something about our worth. Gina has discovered that she misinterpreted her mother's depression as a reflection of her own worth. "I realized I used to think, 'Mommy is spending time in bed because she doesn't want to play with me.' This became a belief that I wasn't worthy of her time." As little kids, feeling unworthy of a parent's time often translates to the idea that we aren't worthy—period.

Noele had a particularly heartbreaking childhood and went on to have a child of her own, under complicated circumstances, who was taken away from her. She's uncovered a voice of unworthiness all her own based on an interpretation of her family's difficulties. She's always told herself, "If I was ever truly worthy, my family would have wanted me, and my daughter could have stayed with me." Finally, she's coming to terms with the fact that her family's inability to care for her was and is not a reflection on her worth.

In my case, I interpreted my ex-husband's behavior through the lens of my own self-worth issues. In my mind, the fact that he didn't work meant I had to buy things for him. Whenever he asked me for something, I felt it was my responsibility to get it. My own inner voice translated the situation into the belief that I didn't deserve to spend much money on myself. Even though he never said, "I won't love you if you don't buy me things," that's what I unconsciously believed, and I felt the pressure.

When we interpret what others are saying as critical, we're often projecting our old beliefs about ourselves onto them. We're so afraid that someone else will feel the same way our parent did, for example, that we think they're judging us even if they aren't. We're so hypervigilant about the possibility of criticism that we even create criticisms that aren't there. Let's say your father told you you'd never amount to anything. Even if someone else makes an innocuous, teasing remark, like "Oh, nice try, but you didn't quite get it!" you immediately attach it to the belief that you'll never amount to anything. And you think this individual believes it, too.

In Exercise #16, you wrote down some of your judgments and why those judgments weren't true. Can you think of any more self-judgments that are based on misinterpretations of what others have said or done? If so, go back to where you wrote your exercise answers and add these judgments so that you don't forget them. Then, add the reasons why the judgments aren't true.

The more we become aware that we're misinterpreting what others think and feel, the more we spare ourselves needless pain. Decide right now that you'll start to notice when you make assumptions about what someone is thinking or feeling about you. Then, check in with yourself. Notice that you're feeling that old belief again, and breathe. Tell yourself, "Oh, that's just the old belief rearing its ugly head again. That's not who I really am." Even if you still can't quite convince yourself that the belief isn't true, repeat, "That's not who I really am." In time—if you keep at it—the truth will win! *Because it really isn't who you are.*

The Voice of Unworthiness

How can you tell if the voice you hear in your head is the negative "voice of unworthiness"? It comes out in distorted or exaggerated language. Here are some examples of "negative-speak" that keeps us stuck at the mercy of limiting beliefs, excuses, and underlying commitments:

1. **Absolutes.** Whenever we speak in black-and-white, all-or-nothing terms, we can be sure that it's negative talk. The words "never" and "always" are big giveaways. "I can't do *anything* right." "I'll *never* make it on my own."

2. **Jumping to Conclusions.** As I said in the previous section, this is when we assume we know what others are thinking, and we assume it's something bad . . . about us. Think again: How many times have you assumed that you didn't receive a reply to an e-mail because the person was mad at you . . . only to find out that they never got it? Or they wrote back, and you didn't get the reply? Or they simply didn't think it was necessary to write back? Or they forgot? Or they were sick?

3. **Defeatist Thinking.** We decide we already know what's going to happen, sometimes based on past

experience. And we're sure what's going to happen won't be good. "I tried to start a business once, and it didn't work out. So I'm sure not going to do that again!" "I couldn't get a job at that company, so why bother?"

4. **Emphasizing the Negative.** If we have a performance review at work with several complimentary remarks, we focus only on the one or two negative statements and discount all of the positive.

5. **"Shoulding" All Over Ourselves.** "I should have done this." "I shouldn't have done that." "I must do better next time." These are the kinds of comments that cause us to feel guilty about our behavior. Yes, you want to increase your self-worth, but the gentler you can be with yourself during the process, the more your self-worth will grow.

6. **Calling Ourselves Names.** Sometimes, we label ourselves as a "loser," a "moron," "stupid," "lame." I know we often use these terms jokingly, but they really can have an impact on our self-worth. If you use them, make sure you don't really mean it! If you *do* mean it, try to catch yourself when you use them, and stop.

The Fear of Worthiness

Some of us have an underlying commitment to unworthiness. Our identity is actually tied to it, and we believe that we're fundamentally unworthy. Why would anyone make a commitment to such a thing? Childhood programming, of course. But this particular commitment is often tenacious, because we're *afraid* of feeling worthy. The secret benefit of the commitment is that it keeps us safe. Think about it: If we dare to believe we're worthy, what if we discover we're wrong? We'd not only feel terrible, but we'd also be humiliated. Choosing to feel unworthy from the start is a preemptive strike. "If I already *know* I'm unworthy, the new kid in the school yard can't hurt me as much when he tells me I'm ugly."

Even if we don't have an underlying commitment to unworthiness, we might have a pervasive belief about worth. One of the beliefs I hear a lot is "I'm not enough, and there isn't enough." That leads to the underlying commitment to deprive ourselves. If there isn't enough, and we're not worthy, that means everyone else gets first dibs. We're afraid to take our rightful portion.

We've already talked quite a bit about how women tend to take care of others first, which often leaves little for themselves. Did your mother do that? If she modeled that for you, it's a big part of your programming.

Pauline says, "So much of my self-worth is based on what's on the 'outside,' rather than how I feel on the inside. I tend to let my husband and close friends have their way almost all the time without even thinking about what I want. I realize now that I don't speak up because I'm afraid of what they'll think of me."

With awareness, Pauline can begin to catch herself, correct her behavior, and make a different choice. Whenever she sees herself starting to take "the short end of the stick," she can stop and say to herself, "No, I'm enough, and there's enough for everyone. I get just as much as everybody else. I deserve to have first dibs. I deserve to say which movie I'd like to see. I deserve to choose the restaurant." It can start as simply as that, and then spiral out into more important areas of her life. Of course, we all have to make compromises and allow everyone in a group to have their say and their piece of the pie. But we certainly deserve to give ourselves equal treatment.

This habit of putting others first also comes out in "the chameleon act." If you're a people-pleaser type like me, you frequently turn yourself—like a chameleon—into what others want and need you to be. Whether that's who you are or not. I still sometimes catch myself wanting to do that. It comes out of the fear that who I am isn't enough, and I'm not worthy of being me.

These days, I'm better able to stop myself from morphing into what somebody else wants. It still takes some effort, but I make it a point to check in with myself to find out what I need, want, feel, and think before I move on to anyone else. This allows me to respond, rather than react, to people and situations. It allows me to be more authentic, and it spares me the resentment I would feel later because I didn't get what I desired.

Heather came to terms with a hidden fearful belief that said, "I'm not enough without stuff." She dug deep and discovered, "I believe fundamentally that I'm less worthy than other people, and therefore should *have* less. But at the same time, I believe that I need *more*, or people will see my unworthiness. If I have nothing on the outside to prove my value, I have no value." Her beliefs are a Catch-22. She feels she isn't worthy of much, so to her having very little means she remains unworthy. What can she do? She can start with the awareness that she's attached her worth to physical objects— rather than who she is. That's a big piece right there. She can also remind herself that if others dismiss her because of her lack of "stuff," that's good information to have. Are they *really* the kind of people she wants in her life?

Often, we women also tend to base our self-worth on our looks. It can be shocking to notice how much of our worth is tied to the way others see us. We're scared that if we aren't thin enough or don't have the right hair or the greatest face, we're not worthy of relationships, friendships, jobs, and money. The media certainly bombards us with images that show women are most valued for how we look.

It isn't easy to counteract such pervasive programming. So the trick is to notice when we get caught up in valuing ourselves based on appearances . . . and say, "Whoa! Hold the phone! I don't want to do that!" Catching ourselves in the act of low self-worth is a big part of the process. The habits are often both tenacious and hidden, so awareness is key.

For other women, worth is tied to their accomplishments and professional successes. As Paige puts it, "I believe I have to prove my worthiness by overachieving, exceeding others' and my own expectations of what I think is possible to achieve." Boy, can I identify with that one!

Yet a lot of the time we diminish and downplay our accomplishments. We act like they're no big deal. Alicia says, "I have a Ph.D. in math education, and I still view it as nothing special. It's something I usually leave out of my story when people ask me about myself." I don't know about you, but I consider having a Ph.D. to be quite an achievement! But she often doesn't even share it with people. This belief that her accomplishments are unimportant has affected her worthiness to such a degree that she even relinquished her inheritance from her parents' estate to her brother. Now, she's working on becoming willing to be worthy of not only claiming her achievements, but giving to herself as much as she has given to others. Again, awareness was the first step to making that change.

Yazmin has a similar story. She has carried the shadow belief her whole life that she "doesn't know how." Yet she's accomplished a great many things over the years, including making a lot of money. It's simply not true that she "doesn't know how," but that belief was engraved on her psyche at a very young age. By applying awareness, her fears of worthiness are gradually dissipating.

All of these self-worth bugaboos are based in fear of what others think of us. Moving away from defining myself based on how others see me has been perhaps the most important aspect of my growth. It isn't like I have no regard for what others think—believe me, I'm still tracking it!—but I don't base my *worth* on their thoughts and feelings.

This, of course, was a gradual process using the tools in this chapter. Today, I'm much more likely to brush off someone else's judgment of me. It doesn't "stick" to me because I know their opinion isn't an accurate reflection of my worth. It's so good to finally know I'm lovable and worthy, no matter what they think! If you don't already know this about yourself, keep reading. You can—and will—develop that kind of self-worth, too. I promise! (Keep reading!)

Clearing Mistakes from the Past

We all make mistakes. Some of your mistakes might even be big ones. But what's happened in the past has nothing to do with your worthiness.

Your worthiness is a function of your presence on this planet as a human being. It has no relationship to what you *do*. It's about who you *are*. As I've said, that one was a big lesson for me! Once I no longer linked my value with my success or failure, I allowed myself to make mistakes. I no longer held myself to the perfectionism that said if I didn't do everything exactly right, it meant I was worthless. Nobody's perfect, so why do we hold ourselves to such standards?

Look, I know that some people can be cruel when you make a mistake. But even if *they* can't be forgiving, *you* can. It's your job to be forgiving of yourself. That's a tough nut sometimes, but the effort will pay off in spades.

If you've made a big mistake, you can apologize and try to make amends for it, as you make new, better choices. Taking responsibility for your actions and saying you're sorry to someone can be a huge step toward increasing your self-worth. It relieves a lot of the guilt you carry that says, "Look what I did. How can I let myself have what I want?" If you feel you need to do more to make amends than just say, "I'm so sorry," by all means do it.

Just stay mindful that you don't punish yourself by paying for any given mistake repeatedly. It can easily become yet another excuse to stay small. Your amends should be equivalent to the offense, but don't let it take over your life. You deserve forgiveness—your own and from others—just for being a fallible, beautiful human being. Keep reminding yourself that we all make mistakes. What matters is the way you show up and take responsibility for them, as well as the choices you make going forward. Start new from who you are today!

Unconditional Love

I said that there's no "ultimate" state of self-worth, and that's true. But if there's an ideal to strive for, it's unconditional love for ourselves and others. Unconditional love is hard for us humans, though. We've been taught through religion and culture that we have to earn our right to be loved. That belief has caused lots of self-worth problems.

What is unconditional love anyway? It's loving, without conditions, regardless of circumstances. You love someone because of who they are, not because of what they do. They don't have to do anything to earn your love. If you're having a hard time grasping that such unconditional love is possible, think about some of the children in your life. It's easy to love kids regardless of their behavior.

So if you love *yourself* unconditionally, you continue to love yourself even when you make a mistake. It's affection without limitation. Accepting yourself as you are without judgment.

Conditional love, on the other hand, ends when you don't accomplish what you'd hoped. Let's say you apply for a bank loan for a new business. You're really excited. Then . . . you don't get the loan. Suddenly, you feel unworthy. Why? Because you attached your self-worth to whether or not you got that loan. Often, we withhold love from ourselves in such situations. But really, who knows if the position would have been as great as you thought? It's certainly not reason to beat yourself up. There's likely something even better for you on the horizon.

When we seek validation from outside of ourselves, it's another sign of our desperation to feel we're worthy. Yet no validation from others will ever do the trick. If our worth is dependent on what others think of us, it's like walking a tightrope. Someone else's bad mood could cause us to take a tumble off that rope.

I have to say it again: Self-worth is an inside job. The truth is that until we love ourselves, we can't fully believe or accept the love of others. Friends, family, and loved ones may indeed love us, but their love won't truly sink in until we believe on the inside that we're worthy of it. This is one of the reasons we hear criticisms more loudly than compliments.

We have to love ourselves, and it needs to be as close to unconditional as we can muster. If it's based on what we do or don't do, it's going to be too fragile to withstand the trials and tests of the human experience. If, on the other hand, you're worthy simply because of who you are, you won't beat yourself up when something doesn't turn out as you'd hoped.

In her book, *Money: A Love Story*, Kate Northrup talks about how money is just love in physical form. As I said in the Introduction, until we feel worthy of love on the inside, we won't feel worthy of money on the outside. Remember: When we don't feel worthy, we perpetuate behaviors that prevent us from allowing more money into our lives.

But don't get me wrong here. For those fellow perfectionists out there, I'm not saying you have to love yourself perfectly 24/7 without ever having another self-judgment for the rest of your life. If you catch yourself saying, "Oh, I'm beating up on myself again. I just can't get this self-worth stuff right!" . . . well, you're falling into the perfectionist trap. No matter how much work we do, there will still be moments when we judge ourselves. It's part of being human!

The key is to stay aware in those moments and to develop an "observer self" who can watch the situation. This part of you can watch as you put yourself down, and offer soothing words to help bring you back to equilibrium. I'll give you some tips later in the chapter about positive self-talk. Developing a regular practice is a huge part of becoming willing to be worthy.

The next time you struggle with unconditional love, think about this: If you looked at a playground full of little kids, how would you know which ones were worthy and which weren't? It's an absurd question—no little kid is unworthy! And that includes *you*.

EXERCISE #17: TRY UNCONDITIONAL LOVE ON FOR SIZE

Let's explore the differences between conditional and unconditional love.

1. Think about the ways you're currently trying to prove your worth. Do you try to prove it by overachieving at work? Do you try to prove it in relationships by putting others first? I tried to prove my worth by being indispensable at work and trying to buy my husband's love. Write down the ways you try to prove your worth at work, at home, with relatives, or with friends.

2. What would it feel like to love yourself unconditionally—not to have to *earn* your worth? What would it feel like to have love in your heart, just for you? Could you still love yourself if you were penniless and had nothing? Close your eyes and really feel what that would be like.

3. Think of the person you love most in the world—perhaps an innocent child whom you feel is 100 percent worthy of love. Now, turn that love back on yourself, and imagine loving yourself that much. Does it feel comfortable or uncomfortable? What would have to shift internally for you to really love yourself that much? What would you have to give up to love yourself unconditionally? Your beliefs about your unworthiness? Write down any thoughts that come to mind.

Keep Moving Past Your "Worth Threshold"

In order to have more, we have to change our thinking, behaviors, and habits related to self-worth—little by little. As we do that, we can continue to increase our "worth threshold." This means that we allow ourselves to receive more and more.

We walk around thinking, "Hey, I will happily let myself receive! Give me the lottery winnings! Show me the money! I have no problem with that." But the truth is that deep down, we *do* have a problem with that. Our self-worth beliefs—which we've always related to as facts—will determine how much we let ourselves have. And that includes money.

We can inch past our current threshold of what we're willing to have by catching ourselves when we perpetuate patterns and behaviors of low self-worth. Here are some strategies for increasing that worth threshold:

1. **Positive Self-Talk.** Listen for self-judgments, and replace them with nurturing self-talk. "I can't believe I could be so stupid" becomes "I did the best I could. It's safe to be imperfect. Nobody else is perfect either. I love myself anyway." When my critical voice starts to shout, I say, "Oh, here you are again. I've been expecting you, and I'm going to turn your volume down now. We're not doing that anymore."

   When you practice nurturing, loving self-talk, you can more easily elicit compassion for yourself by talking to the small child within. How can you beat up on yourself if you're relating to your young, vulnerable self? And in truth, the part of you that feels stupid really is that young, vulnerable child.

2. **Stop Yourself.** As I've said more than once, one of the best strategies to stop poor self-worth habits in their tracks is simply *moment-to-moment awareness or mindfulness.* Once you become mindful of behaviors and patterns that aren't in keeping with the self-worth you desire, you can begin to catch yourself in the act. For example, the next time you put someone else's needs ahead of your own, you can stop and ask yourself what *you* want. The next time you tell yourself, "I can't," you can say, "Wait a minute. Is it true that I can't? What do I really want here? If I want this, what's holding me back? What am I really afraid of? Can I talk myself down from my fears and still go after what I want?"

3. **Look Around You.** As I've already said, your outer life is a reflection of the state of your inner self-worth. So look around. Does your environment reflect someone with the high self-worth you're after? If not, how can you change your environment to be closer to what you deserve? Now, I'm aware that you may not necessarily be able to go out and buy a beautiful home tomorrow. You might need to do some real work on your self-worth before you could make that happen. But you can make small changes in the interim. It might be as simple as cleaning more often, fixing something you've let go for a long time, or sprucing the place up in whatever ways you can. When you do

something nice for yourself, you might feel your self-worth increase, and you can build on that.

Jeanine, for example, has a "cheap" habit that's a direct reflection of her self-worth. "If I let myself buy new clothes, they have to be from a very cheap store, and usually on sale. A treat is buying myself a $3 bottle of wine. Perhaps being cheap with yourself cheapens you. I want to feel worthy and capable of full-price and even luxury items without guilt." I don't advocate anyone spending beyond their means, but often, we buy cheap items because we don't feel we deserve better. While staying within your budget, allow yourself to have something really nice now and then. As your self-worth increases, so will your net worth. Then, you can treat yourself more often. And eventually with higher ticket items, if you so desire.

4. **Bragging Rights.** Get yourself a "boasting buddy," and share your successes without shame. It's important to have people in your life who are happy for you when good things happen. We have a fear that others will feel jealous, but if they do, that's their issue to resolve. Some people even try to bring us down when we experience something great. It's their own lack of self-worth at play, though, so feel compassion for them, if you can. Then, when you find yourself feeling jealous of others, remind yourself that if they can do it, so can you. Their success is only an indication that it can be done. You aren't excluded from that success unless you allow yourself to be.

5. **Your Own Personal Cheerleader.** Besides being a "boasting buddy," ask that friend (or someone else) to be your personal cheerleader. Then, offer to reciprocate. In this role, you and your friend will give each other self-worth pep talks when you find that you're getting down on yourselves. Give each other reality checks about self-judgments. Encourage each other to step past your fears and go for what you really desire. Hold each other accountable for any action steps you set. Just make a rule that no negativity is allowed, and any pushing toward your goals should be gentle, not forceful.

6. **Find a Community.** The main reason I started my coaching groups is so that my clients could cheer one another on. It has turned out to be more powerful than my wildest dreams. Through our weekly calls and private Facebook groups, my clients are helping each other in unbelievable ways. We soothe one another during the hard times and pat each other on the back when something goes well. If you can find such a community, you'll be amazed at the results. If you can't find one, *create one*—either to meet in person or online. Once again, just have a rule in place that no negativity is allowed!

It's easy to forget that increasing self-worth is a gradual and lifelong process. So keep that front of mind! Because even as you expand your worthiness threshold, you'll still have to deal with those old demons that occasionally rise up. Over time, they'll become quieter, and you'll pay less attention to them. But every time you expand beyond your current threshold, you can expect them to pipe up again. Don't worry; it's just the voice of fear, in a misguided attempt to keep you safe.

You'll also continue to find blind spots. Here's one of mine: My husband got our truck in the divorce, which left me without a car. Believe it or not, I lived in Boulder, Colorado, for three years with only a bicycle. Then, a friend said, "What do you mean you don't have a car?" I said, "My ex-husband got the truck in the divorce"—as if that was the only vehicle in the world! For some reason, I just hadn't believed I was worthy of spending money on a car of my own, even though I could afford one.

When I finally discovered my blind spot (took me three years—duh!), I bought a car . . . and paid for it outright. A new car wasn't a necessity, but I wanted it—and I was finally willing to let myself have exactly the car I wanted. That car became a symbol of my independence—the freedom to go where I wanted, when I wanted. It was a lot of money to spend, and I had to take few deep breaths before writing that check! But giving myself permission was all about letting go of the belief that I deserved deprivation—and about believing in my own worth instead.

So you'll move into greater self-worth one step at a time. You'll discover new blind spots. And that awareness will propel you forward to take whatever steps you deem necessary to have what you desire. Sometimes it may go slower than you'd like, but be patient. Pat yourself on the back every time you catch yourself in an old habit or change a behavior. Catch yourself, too, if you beat up on yourself for backsliding. Use that as yet another opportunity to have compassion for yourself and stoke your self-worth.

Giving and Receiving

In the last section, I mentioned that we receive only what we feel we're worthy of receiving. So how do you work on your ability to receive more?

First, through observing your "receiving habits." When you get a gift, how do you feel? If someone does you a favor, do you immediately feel that you have to reciprocate?

Practice receiving as though you deserve it (because, as we covered earlier in this chapter, you do!). You don't have to reciprocate. If you have a chance to do something for the giver at some point, and your heart feels full of desire to do so, go for it. But reciprocating out of obligation is a habit directly related to low self-worth.

When *you* give a gift, are you doing so in order to get something equal in return? If you're like me, giving a gift is a joy in and of itself. In a certain way, the sense of delight we get from giving is a gift the receiver gives *us*, just by . . . *receiving*! Would you want to deny such a pleasure to others? I didn't think so!

Conversely, if you feel that people do owe you when you give them a gift, examine where that belief comes from. Are you unconsciously setting up the same obligation when you receive gifts? Practice giving without any price tag attached. Allow the gift to be emotionally clean, with nothing expected in return. Experience the joy of giving for its own sake. Then try receiving from that same place. Allow yourself to accept more from others—and from the universe at large—because that nasty sense of obligation will no longer be attached.

Just for a moment, imagine what it would feel like to receive wondrous gifts from others and from the universe with no requirement to give back. You deserve these gifts, and they're being given to you simply because you're you.

Can you allow yourself to experience that? What does it feel like?

Worthiness Mentors

After I left my marriage and began to dismantle the belief that my self-worth was contingent on being perfect and doing things for others, my good friend Patty took me shopping. This was *huge* for me—I rarely spent money on myself, and shopping was my least favorite activity. But Patty was resolute, ferrying me to Donna Karan's Urban Zen store in New York. Let me tell you—the price tags in that store made my eyeballs pop out! Patty has a healthy sense of self-worth, has no problem spending money on herself, and always looks fabulously stylish. That day she became a "worthiness mentor" for me. I ended up spending more on myself than I've ever spent in my life. It was weird but liberating, and it was the start of a new way of being for me. In this new version of Nancy, I accept that I'm worthy of nice things.

I can't recommend enough that you look for your own worthiness mentors. These are not necessarily like your cheerleaders, your community, or your boasting buddies. These are people who have what you want when it comes to money, lifestyle, and presence. They're people you admire, who have the qualities you want to develop in yourself. If it's someone who's a good friend (or capable of becoming a good friend), this individual might take you by the hand, the way Patty did for me. If not, take the opportunity to treat the experience as a research process—ask this person questions about what they do and how they think. Then, take notes!

Realize, too, that you *already have* the qualities you see in these other people. You wouldn't be able to recognize their gifts unless they were resonating inside of you—dormant maybe, but itching to pop out! Having a great mentor can help you get in touch with those qualities inside you and let them spring forward.

The Intersection of Self-Worth and Net Worth

In Step Three, we worked primarily on beliefs related to money—and how they become intertwined with our self-worth. In this chapter, we've focused primarily on beliefs related directly to self-worth. One of the most important lessons I learned after I went out on my own is that self-worth and net worth are proportional. When I increased my self-worth enough to pursue my dreams, I automatically increased my net worth. What a surprise it was to see that I could grow my net worth *outside* of a full-time job! Of course, I'm not the first person who's done that, but so many of us have a hard time believing it's possible.

The truth is that whatever your beliefs about your worthiness, they will directly affect the amount of financial ease you can create in your life. As I've said, this is the main reason some people find that the "law of attraction" becomes blocked or hits a ceiling. No matter how many exercises they do to become magnetic and abundant, their financial situation remains the same. Deep unconscious beliefs about self-worth are the missing pieces of the puzzle.

It's up to us to take the actions necessary to clear these obstacles. And it's a lifelong journey. You'll never get bored because there will always be more to learn about yourself. We're nothing if not wonderfully complex beings.

Yes, it takes work to get past the programming of our childhoods. But it isn't a burden. It's something to cherish and relish. As adults, we have a wonderful opportunity. We can choose to base our identities on who we truly are inside—the personality, the essence we came into this life with.

This is who you were before you were imprinted with anybody else's opinions—imperfect, human, thoroughly beautiful, and oh so worthy. Trust me: There's so much more possible for you, and self-worth is the key! All you have to do is turn it, and the door will open.

EXERCISE #18: BURN THE NEGATIVE AND BASK IN THE POSITIVE

For this exercise, you'll need several actual loose pieces of paper. A screen or journal alone won't work for this one. You'll also need matches or a lighter and a safe way to burn some of the paper. Have your journal or computer/tablet available, too, though, in case you want to use it for the final part of the exercise.

1. On one of the pieces of paper, write down the three most important desires in your life that you don't yet feel you deserve. You might start with something like, "I don't yet feel I'm worthy of having my own business."

2. On a second piece of paper, write down what you would have to give up to be worthy of these desires. Would you have to give up a difficult relationship, a job, a sense of belonging with your family, or simply an old negative belief? What would you have to let go of?

3. Light the second piece of paper on fire, and allow it to burn to ash. If you aren't ready to let go of all of those things, you can transfer what you *can* let go of

right now onto another piece of paper, and burn that by itself.

4. Stop for a moment, and take in the fact that you've just burned some of the obstacles to your desires. Take a deep breath!

5. To finish on a positive note, write down all the compliments you can remember that you've ever received. These can be compliments about anything. You might want to put this list on your computer or tablet so that you'll always have it handy. Continue to add to it as you think of more compliments. Whenever your self-worth wanes, pull out this list and read it.

Affirm Your Worth

"I am unconditionally worthy of all that I desire."

TAKE BACK YOUR FINANCIAL POWER

"Our position is that you aren't going to pay your husband any maintenance," my divorce lawyer told me. "He's healthy and able to earn a living. He's just choosing not to."

Then, the day of mediation came, and the mediator told us that my husband's lawyer was making financial demands for a seven-year period. I expected my attorney to flat-out refuse, as we had discussed. Instead, he made a counteroffer and started to negotiate for a shorter maintenance period.

What? We'd agreed there would be *no* maintenance! My lawyer and I hadn't even talked about what I would consider a fair settlement. How could he negotiate without knowing my wishes? I was dumbstruck.

What should I have done in that moment? Well . . . I *should* have stopped the conference then and there and asked the mediator to leave for a few minutes. Then, I should have talked strategy with my attorney. My first question should have been: "Why did you start negotiating after you told me our position was no maintenance at all?" The attorney was working for *me*, after all. I was paying him to do what I asked.

But what did I do instead? I sat there paralyzed and silent. I just allowed the mediator and my lawyer to negotiate without my input, while I gave away my financial power.

It took an experience *that* painful to teach me an important lesson: I have the absolute right to say what's going to happen with my money. Why would I allow someone else to give it away without my approval? But that's exactly what I did. I was afraid to challenge my lawyer. I thought he knew what he was doing, and I didn't think I was smart enough to understand the situation. Mostly, I didn't want anyone to think I was stupid. (There was that fear again!) And I didn't want to waste anyone's time by pausing the process. Bottom line: I didn't speak up because I didn't feel worthy.

As a result, I don't think my divorce settlement was fair to me. But I have no one to blame but myself, since I didn't own my power and state what I really wanted.

The woman I am now would *never* allow my attorney to take over a negotiation and give away more than I thought was just. I would speak up and say, "Wait a minute! This isn't acceptable!"

What created this shift in me? My newfound voice is a direct consequence of becoming willing to be worthy—by walking through the same steps you have in front of you in this book. In Step Two, you already admitted who (or what) holds the purse strings in your life. Now, because you've completed Steps Three through Six, you're ready to go further. Step Seven is *Take Back Your Financial Power*.

There are lots of different ways we can inadvertently give away our financial power. It can be a matter of handing over the purse strings long-term to someone else—as we discovered in Step Two—or you may give them to someone in a short-term way, as in the example of my divorce negotiation. You may have handed the power over to your family, or to a limiting belief that's held you hostage since childhood. You might discover that you've given power away for years without realizing it. That's because through the lens of low self-worth, we often stay blind to the places in our lives where we hand over our power. When the blinders finally come off, it can be downright shocking to discover how much we've tolerated over the course of our lives.

What if you're in a traditional marriage, where he takes care of all the finances while you take care of the house? Again, if it's working for you, that's a perfectly acceptable arrangement. But as I've said, it's important to make sure you maintain your financial power even *within* that arrangement. If your agreement with your husband is that you ask his permission to spend money, your financial power is solely in his hands, not your own. Have a discussion about obtaining funds of your own for the work you do around the house. Then, you can start a "Me Fund"—your own account with your own money, even if the rest of your finances are held jointly. You'll feel that you've *earned* the money you spend on yourself, and you can buy what you need and want without guilt.

The more worthy we feel, the more we become aware of the injustice of powerlessness. Then, we simply refuse to allow anyone or anything to control our money and how we handle it. We want to own what's rightfully ours because we know, without question, that we deserve it.

It's 10:00 P.M.—Do You Know Where Your Accounts Are?

My client Sheila has a cautionary tale for us all. "Since I've been with my husband, money has never been an issue. I could do pretty much whatever I wanted. Now, I've learned we're getting deeper and deeper into a financial hole. Turns out he was doing all the worrying for me and didn't really share what was going on with our finances," she says.

Unfortunately, her husband wasn't managing their money nearly as well as she thought. There were a number of problems that he kept from her in an effort to protect her.

In Tonya's case, she found that by relying on her husband to make all the money in her marriage, she had no drive to succeed on her own. "It enabled me to stay put and be safe and stay in my comfort zone," she says. In short, she gave away her power. "Bottom line," she says, "being taken care of was fear-based and enabled me to hide behind all the things I had on the outside—the 'stuff' I was able to buy. No one had to see the real me, and I didn't have to be responsible for possibly failing."

Even if we're responsible for the home, while our partner is responsible for the finances, it's up to us to take part in money matters. By the same token, our partner should know how the home is run. If either partner becomes ill (or God forbid, even worse), the other should know how to handle everything from the washing machine to the investment accounts.

Marlene's father relied on his wife to take care of almost everything, including their finances. When his wife was diagnosed with a debilitating illness in their later years, he not only didn't know where she kept his underwear, but he had actually forgotten how to write a check! When we relinquish responsibility, we create all sorts of financial problems—problems that can turn into excuses, holding us back from getting what we want. To be in a powerful partnership, both people need to know how to balance a checkbook, pay the bills, maintain the retirement accounts, and so on. It's important to know where all of our financial records live, and to be aware of all bank accounts, login details, balances, and investments.

If you don't already have access to this information, don't delay! And if you fear that your spouse or financial advisor isn't making sound choices, get another opinion. In other words, as we discussed in Step One, take off the blinders! That's what financial power looks like.

EXERCISE #19: WHERE'S THE POWER?

In Step Two, you explored who and what holds the purse strings in your life. Let's take it further and look at all areas of your financial life one by one.

1. For each of these items, answer "yes" if you feel you hold the financial power in this area and "no" if you don't. By financial power, I mean, do you know account numbers and amounts? Do you know where the accounts are located? Do you know the approximate balances of the accounts? Do you have access to the account statements—without permission? If you do have to ask permission, please answer "no."

Checking account(s)	Yes__	No__	N/A__
Savings account(s)	Yes__	No__	N/A__
Investments	Yes__	No__	N/A__
Mortgage account(s)	Yes__	No__	N/A__
Retirement account(s)	Yes__	No__	N/A__
Trust(s)	Yes__	No__	N/A__
Property	Yes__	No__	N/A__
Business(es)	Yes__	No__	N/A__
Estate matters	Yes__	No__	N/A__

2. If you answered "yes" to everything, congratulations! You can skip past the rest of this exercise. If you answered "no" to some of the items, don't fret. But please do continue with the exercise. For each of those items, if it's another person who has control of

the information, can you set a date and time to discuss the accounts with that person? If it's your spouse or partner, you can say that you think it's important to have the information in case anything happens to them. You can explain that you want to be prepared and that you want to feel that you have an equal say in financial matters. Assure him/her that you aren't going to pull money out of any of the accounts without first consulting them.

3. If it's scary to think about discussing information and access to the accounts, make a list of your "what ifs." What frightens you about asking for equal access? For example, "What if he gets mad?" "What if he threatens to leave me?" If you answer the "what if" questions, the worst-case scenarios in this case can be pretty scary. If you feel, for example, that your husband would indeed leave you if you took back your financial power, only you can decide what you want and need to do. Only you can determine what your heightened self-worth requires for your life.

4. If it's a "what," not a "who," that keeps you from having your financial power—a belief, an excuse, or an underlying commitment—write down your "what ifs" related to fears of looking at your accounts. What's the worst-case scenario for each? While the worst cases might not be pleasant, remember that you can begin to alter those possible future scenarios by changing your behavior now. If you don't have a retirement account or a trust, for example, write down your "what ifs" about creating each kind of account or legal document that might be a good idea for you.

5. If you're able to successfully get the information and access to your accounts, or take a look at them when you've been afraid to look, pat yourself on the back. You have taken back a big piece of your financial power. You

no longer have to worry that you won't be able to take care of matters if something catastrophic happens. Just knowing where everything is will give you a great sense of ease. Of course, now that you've gotten the information, don't turn a blind eye again. Continue to check the accounts regularly. If you worry that you might fall back into your old habits, put a reminder on your calendar to check your accounts on a monthly basis.

End the "Head in the Sand" Syndrome

If the idea of keeping regular track of your accounts still feels scary—or like something you'll never do—you probably have what I call the "head in the sand" syndrome. It's the opposite of financial power. When we don't break this habit, it can wreak some serious havoc in our lives.

Sheila sure found that out the hard way. Giving all of her financial power away to her husband meant the household was in jeopardy—and she didn't know until the damage had been done. Perhaps if she had known, she could have helped him make better decisions.

I've seen many high-performing women—women making plenty of money—who have "head in the sand" syndrome. They're intimidated by the thought of balancing their checkbooks. They don't open their bank statements or bills. Then, none of it is handled and late fees accrue. Sometimes, the electricity gets turned off even though they can afford to pay the bill! At the very least, the bills don't get paid until the last minute because procrastination is the natural result of having your head in the sand.

What causes this malady? Again, we're afraid of what we don't know, so we hide. We're afraid of what we might find out, so we look the other way and hope it will all just go away. But our finances are our own responsibility—full stop. Even if we aren't as financially educated as our partner or our lawyer or our accountant, the financial decisions they make on our behalf are still our responsibility. If they offer advice, we need to ask questions. We need to look at the numbers. We need to know about the decisions being made in our households, regardless of who's making them.

There's nothing powerful about not wanting to see reality. So what can we do about this psychological block? How can we stop the procrastination and develop the courage to look—powerfully—at our financial situation? How can we then do what needs to be done to make it better? Here are some tips:

1. **Alter the due dates.** If you put off paying your bills every month, for example, look into altering the due dates. You can usually ask your creditors to make the due dates when you request. If cash flow isn't a problem, make all the due dates the same day so you can take care of them all in one fell swoop. If you can't pay every bill at once, stagger the due dates to coincide with your paychecks. Then, put in your calendar a nonnegotiable time for paying your bills—a date and time you know you can keep.

2. **Get some software.** Try Mint financial software for free or, if you can afford it, get Quicken or QuickBooks to help you keep up with the numbers. This software can make balancing your

bank account much easier. It does most of the work for you.

3. **Hire a bookkeeper.** Again, if you can afford it, consider hiring a bookkeeper to help you keep track of your finances. That way your bank statement won't go unbalanced and your bills won't go unopened or unpaid.

4. **Make it fun for yourself!** Whatever money-related task you're trying to get yourself to do, make it fun! Have your favorite tea or a glass of wine, light a candle, and play your favorite music. Make up a silly song about paying your bills, and sing it to yourself as you write the checks or hit the "pay now" button on each website.

5. **Give yourself a prize.** When you're finished, reward yourself for a job well done. It can be as simple as taking a bath or a quiet walk. Just make it something you sincerely enjoy, and allow yourself to feel good about taking back this piece of your financial power.

6. **Get a buddy.** If you just can't seem to get yourself to take care of some important financial matter, enlist a friend to keep you accountable. He or she might sit with you while you pay your bills, balance your checkbook, or do your taxes. Your friend might offer you moral support as you deal with writing a will. You could even get together with a friend for a bill-paying party. If you can concentrate with a movie running at the same time, turn it on, pop some popcorn, and open a bottle of wine. Just find a way to keep the task from being such a drudge.

The bottom line is try everything—nurturing self-talk, a buddy, a coach or therapist, a financial advisor, turning financial chores into fun, giving yourself a reward after you take care of an issue—whatever it takes. As long as you hide from what needs to be done, you'll also be hiding from your financial power.

The State of Your Estate

Millie's cousin, Craig, amassed a small fortune into the millions of dollars. When he suddenly became ill in his 60s, he realized he'd never made a will. At the last minute, he hired an attorney who helped him construct a will on his deathbed. When it came time for probate, however, it was clear that the will had not been properly thought out.

The biggest problem was that Craig didn't know how much he was worth. In fact, they found stock certificates lying haphazardly on the floor throughout his home. He owned businesses and property and had never hired a financial advisor to help him keep track of everything. His net worth was anyone's guess. Since Craig was single and childless, he left a certain amount of money in his will to each of his first cousins. Besides the need to figure out how many cousins there were and whether he even had enough money for all of them, there were mistakes made in the will's construction. (Mistakes are a lot more likely when a will is written in a rush.) All of this caused it to go into litigation. In the meantime, all sorts of people came out of the woodwork claiming to be Craig's cousins.

It took years for the whole mess to be sorted out. In the end, there wasn't enough money for each cousin to get the amount Craig had hoped. They all still got a nice chunk of change once the list of actual cousins was established. But the moral of the story is that putting off the writing of your will can be a nightmare for the people left behind.

Even people with very little money can leave big messes for their loved ones to clean up. Adam's parents refused to do any estate planning, so their house remained in both their names. When his mother went into a nursing home on Medicaid, his father was allowed to stay in the house. But then, his father died before his mother, and the house immediately transferred to her. This meant that she was no longer eligible for Medicaid benefits, and the house had to be sold immediately to pay for her nursing care. If the house had been put in Adam's name, he wouldn't have been forced to sell it and use the proceeds.

I know I said I wasn't going to give you tangible financial advice like other financial books would do. But I'm going to break my rule one last time because estate planning is such an important subject. Nobody wants to think about illness or death. But when we avoid taking care of our estate matters, we leave a terrible aftermath for our loved ones.

If you have children, it's especially important to have a will and to find out what other estate planning is a good idea for you, such as trusts, living wills, and health care proxies. People need to know your wishes for your own body, as well as your finances. This will reduce legal problems and fighting among relatives. Trust me: Your kids or whoever is left behind will thank you for having everything in order. Their lives will be so much easier.

Taking care of your estate is one more way that you can exert your financial power and responsibility. Suze Orman has created an incredibly affordable online product called Must Have Documents that provides you with everything you need to get your will and trust in order. I highly recommend it. (There is more information about this in the Resources section at the end of the book.)

Fear of Taking Responsibility

Taking responsibility for our finances is the cornerstone of financial power. In Step Two, we talked about the dangers of *not* taking responsibility. My client Faye learned that lesson in a painful way. "Overall, I like to consider myself a strong and empowered woman, but through this work, I've discovered that I have a serious money shadow. I've repeatedly given away my financial power to the men I've been with, letting them make all the decisions and control the purse strings. The funny thing is, I didn't even know I was doing it! I've always been a hard worker, taking care of business, and going for the gold in whatever my endeavor—but I also have had a long history of attracting wealthy partners, getting comfortable, and handing over the reins of financial responsibility after our relationship became established. This pattern hasn't exactly panned out well."

Recently, she left her nine-to-five job to start a new business. The move shifted the balance of financial power in her relationship, which proved to be a problem. "I found myself having to ask him for money and explain to him exactly what it was to be used for—experiences that left me feeling sheepish and disempowered," she says. "As time passed, we both grew impatient and increasingly resentful of the financial arrangement. He didn't like having to pay for things, and I didn't like having to ask. Yet I felt stuck because I'd chosen to walk away from guaranteed income while birthing my business—on the promise of his assistance." The discomfort of the situation eventually led to their separation and the evaporation of the financial support she'd counted on.

By evaluating her beliefs, excuses, and underlying commitments, Faye has come to realize that she's been "scared to death" of taking back her financial power.

Why? Often, when we fear our power, what we're really afraid of is taking responsibility. It's another big "what if": "What if I take responsibility for my own finances and discover I can't do it right? What if I mess it up?"

When we don't take responsibility for our own money, we put ourselves in a childlike position and let others take care of us. It sets up a parent/child energetic pattern. Once we've reached adulthood, that isn't a healthy pattern to perpetuate with anyone, not even our parents. If the parent/child pattern is with a spouse, it's especially unhealthy for the relationship. On the surface, being taken care of may look very attractive. It might even feel like an even exchange to give away our financial power for safety, security, and love. But that safety, security, and love come at a high price. It means we don't have a say in what happens to us financially. We're at the mercy of someone else. Only when we're responsible for our own financial situation do we have the opportunity to change it.

Every time you take responsibility for a financial matter—even something you deem to be small—you send a message to the universe that you're responsible enough to handle more money when it comes. I know someone who's always late because he says he doesn't have anything important enough to show up on time for. But you have to show up on time to prove you can handle something important enough to be there for! If you take back your financial power, you prove that you're capable of having more money.

As you take responsibility in the area of your finances, you may be surprised at times by what you find yourself doing. In my situation, there came a time when I was no longer required, per our divorce agreement, to pay the mortgage and home owners association dues for the condo where my ex-husband had been living for three years. Since the loan was in my name, he just assumed that I'd continue paying, even though our agreement was complete. He was relating to me as if I were the same woman I'd been in our marriage—scared to death of ruining her credit, and willing to bail him out no matter what. I'm sure it was inconceivable to him that I'd changed as much as I had.

I knew I wasn't going to continue to pay, but I also wanted to educate myself about what would happen to my credit if I didn't. So I spoke to Suze Orman, since we were friends through my work at Hay House. To my surprise, she said, "F*ck your credit! Your self-worth is more important than your net worth." That's right—in this case, taking my power back meant allowing the mortgage to default and go into foreclosure, putting my credit rating in jeopardy. Which is exactly what I did. My ex-husband was furious, of course, but my responsibility was to my own financial power—and my own integrity.

The incident has indeed affected my credit score, although not as much as you might expect. Ironically, though, when I recently received a letter turning me down for credit, I didn't feel ashamed. I was actually proud of myself for finally cutting the financial ties with my ex-husband and taking back my power. I had done the internal work to feel worthy of my value as defined by *me*, not something external like my credit score.

So you see, there may be times when what's actually powerful is counterintuitive. Check in with your gut instincts: What would feel most powerful to you? What would a person with high self-worth do? Then, make the best decision you can.

EXERCISE #20: TAKE RESPONSIBILITY

1. Make a list of any financial circumstances in your life right now where you feel powerless or like a victim. These may have to do with someone else holding the purse strings, or they may simply be situations that you have felt powerless to change. For example, "I feel like a victim of my husband's control of our money," or "I feel powerless to increase my income."

2. Add to your list any financial situations in which you would greatly benefit from taking more responsibility. For example, "I would benefit from taking more responsibility for our family's investment accounts," or "I would benefit from taking responsibility for learning how to market a business of my own."

3. On a scale of 1 to 10, rate the level of responsibility you're currently taking for each of the circumstances you wrote down. One stands for no responsibility, and 10 stands for total responsibility.

4. For each of these circumstances, answer these questions: "What would taking responsibility for this situation look like? What would I have to do to take responsibility here? What would it cost me—financially, emotionally, or in my relationships—to take responsibility here?" Stay open to whatever comes to mind, and write down your thoughts.

5. Allow yourself to feel what it would be like to step out of the role of victim and into your financial power, taking full responsibility for each of these circumstances.

Does it feel great? Does it feel scary? Does it feel a little of both? Write down what you experience.

6. Based on your vision of responsibility, identify what you believe would be the best first action to take in each situation, and write it down. You will revisit this list in Step Eight.

The Blame Game

One of the reasons we frequently hand over responsibility for our finances is that if we don't know what's going on, we don't have to take the blame if something goes wrong. Instead, we can blame whoever was holding the purse strings. In my situation, it wasn't until I took responsibility for the choices I made that I was able to stop blaming my ex-husband for what had happened between us. After all, he never forced me to buy him things, and the attorney didn't force me to hand over more in the divorce settlement than I thought was right. I had to take responsibility for all of that. It was my own lack of self-worth—not another person—that was to blame.

As poet Joseph Brodsky once said, "A pointed finger is a victim's logo—the opposite of the V-sign [victory sign] and a synonym for surrender." By pointing the finger at someone else, we actually surrender our power.

When we blame someone else, we get to feel self-righteous. Sandra realized that she was stuck in the excuse of blaming her ex-husband for not paying enough child support. Certainly, she should stand up for herself and her kids. But she has started to realize that if her ex-husband is financially irre-sponsible and unable to pay, fighting him is like beating a dead horse. Sure, she can hope for a new outcome, while bracing for the next time he disappoints her—yet again. But now she knows that she must either take action to get him to provide more child support, or move on and take responsibil-ity for her own future—regardless of what he does or doesn't do. When she accepts the reality of "what is" in this situation, she'll no longer be tied to expectations or blind hope. She'll stop using her ex-husband's behavior as an excuse to avoid positive action on her own behalf.

Penny's Story

"I'm a stay-at-home mom," says my client Penny. "To me, it's the most important and honorable job that exists. It's a combination of cheerleader, project manager, taxi cab driver, personal advocate, therapist, finance guru, nurse, and chef—all rolled into one huge responsibility that's paid the sum of zero dollars. But who can put a price tag on taking care of and nurturing the lives that you've created?

"I volunteered at church and school. I planted organic gardens. I made Halloween costumes. I baked. I cleaned. I handled all of the family finances. I shopped for bargains. And through it all, I was never questioned about how or when I spent money. All of our accounts were joint, so there was no allowance or penny-pinching on the part of my husband. There was only complete love and support from a man whose only goal was for me to be happy.

"Yet I lived with a small voice in the back of my head that said all of the money I spent wasn't really my money. It was *his* money. And this led to guilt every time I bought something for myself or bought something that didn't perfectly align with how my husband would spend. None of these thoughts were overt, but they accumulated over time and began to erode my self-confidence and diminish my own passions. I found it a struggle to speak up and ask for what I wanted, even in matters that weren't financial in nature. Putting everyone else's needs and opinions before mine became chronic.

"Then, one day, I met Nancy. Together we began a journey that would help me remember my true passion and would erase the shame around my gifts. Since the start of that journey, I've begun my own business centered on what makes my soul sing. It allows me complete flexibility in scheduling my time. I can honor my belief in the importance of being an engaged and involved mom, while also honoring my personal gifts, supporting others, and earning my own money!

"I'd thought that contributing financially to my family wasn't necessary, as long as we were making ends meet. But what I experienced after being paid for doing something that brings me joy was *empowerment*. It's this feeling of empowerment that's shifting everything in my life. It's allowing me to speak up, set boundaries, and confidently move toward a tangible vision that was previously reserved only for my dreams."

Financial Power and Self-Worth

The picture of high self-worth and financial power looks like this: We don't allow anyone else to take money from us that we don't freely give. We know where our accounts reside, we know the account numbers, and we keep track of the balances. Our estate is in order so that the people we leave behind will find it easy to take care of our affairs. We don't allow ourselves to fill emotional emptiness with spending, and we don't allow fears to cause us to hoard money. We stay balanced, competent, and focused around our finances. We own them—they don't own us.

Now, that may seem like a tall order! Like perfection. But no, it isn't about being perfect. We all slip up now and then. What we're striving for is *progressive financial healing*. The idea is just to become aware of where and when you give your power away, so you can begin to bring it back to the person it truly belongs to—you.

EXERCISE #21: YOUR PERSONAL PICTURE OF POWER

1. Write down what financial power would look like in your world. If you had true financial power, what specifically would you do differently? What would change in your life?

2. What's holding you back from making the changes necessary to own your financial power? Write it down.

3. In writing down the picture of your financial power, have you discovered any new places in which you need to take back your power? If so, can you think of a way to regain that power, even if it's just one action step in the right direction? Write down your thoughts.

4. Finally, how would it *feel* to own 100 percent of your financial power? Do any fears come to the surface? Can you allow yourself to feel confident in your ability to handle the power? Can you imagine what it would feel like to have no fear of your power? How does it feel to

be powerful and confident? How does it feel to fully hold the purse strings of your life? Write down your thoughts.

Affirm Your Worth

*"I hold the financial power in my life, and
I'm confident in my power because I deserve it."*

MAKE ONE POWERFUL FINANCIAL DECISION

"What if she asks me to do something scary? What if she shames me for the way I've handled my money? What if she has me invest my money, and I lose it all, ending up with nothing?" Those were the "what ifs" that came up for me when I hired my financial advisor, Melissa Sweet. She had come highly recommended by my dear friend, fellow author and speaker Cheryl Richardson, so I knew I was in good hands. But the fears still rose to the surface to spook me.

My self-worth issues came up, too, as I thought, "Who am I to have a financial advisor?" I still held the belief "Only people with tons of money and investments use financial advisors." During our first conversation on Skype, Melissa asked me to share my money story. When I got to the part about my marriage and my divorce, I broke down. In fact, I spent the entire remainder of the session bawling my eyes out! I still felt such shame about how much I had given my financial power away to my ex-husband and to my lawyer. I even felt ashamed for not knowing what I didn't know. But there's no reason I should have known about finance unless I had studied it. What an unfair expectation I put on myself!

Luckily, Melissa sat patiently and listened to me cry about my financial past. I suppose it wasn't the first time she's experienced a client having an emotional meltdown. If money weren't an emotional issue for you, too, you probably wouldn't be reading this book.

I'm so glad I went through all that because hiring Melissa was a *huge* step for me. She completely changed the way I handled my money. As I've mentioned, I'd been stockpiling all of my savings in a low-interest account—which was almost the equivalent of keeping a pile of cash under my mattress. It helped me feel safe to have that big number in the bank, but in truth, it was just my version of head in the sand syndrome. It wasn't the wisest or most lucrative place to keep that money. I also didn't realize that paying off my mortgage could actually be an investment.

Making that one powerful financial decision—to consult an advisor—changed my life in a number of positive ways. I learned more about the world of finance, got control of my purse strings, and grew my self-worth all at the same time. (Thanks, Melissa!)

What about you? Now that you have an idea of what you want, it's time to take action toward the future that you've envisioned for yourself. And that starts with Step Eight: *Make One Powerful Financial Decision*!

One decision can create a big shift in your life and propel you forward. Even just one small forward movement can cause a positive ripple effect. This step often impacts us in ways we can't predict, or may not even fully recognize at first.

Sally made a surprising change. Even though she was going through financial difficulties, she still spent $100 a month on fake nails. Through this process, she realized how much that expense was adding up and let her nails go au naturel. What she discovered was that the fake nails had been covering up a secret nail-biting habit. Without the camouflage, she became motivated to stop biting her nails— and succeeded!

Remember Michele from the Introduction? Just getting up the courage to ask her financial advisor to put a certain amount of money in her account every month empowered her to stop a long-time eating disorder.

Taking action can dissipate our anxiety, give us more confidence, and change the course of our lives for the better in a myriad of ways. Are you excited? What action will *you* take?

EXERCISE #22: HOLD YOUR OWN PURSE STRINGS

In Exercise #6 (Step Two), you reviewed a list of actions that you might take to regain control of your purse strings. You were asked not to take action at that time because you wouldn't have cleared enough of your shadow beliefs, excuses, and underlying commitments to make it stick. You wouldn't have done the self-worth exercises yet either. Now, assuming you've cleared enough obstacles to your self-worth and strengthened it significantly, you can take action.

1. Review the notes you made in Exercise #6 regarding the statements below, including the personal statements you added to the list. Mark the ones that *could* be a choice for your one powerful financial decision. Feel free to pick more than one because you aren't going to make your final choice until the end of the chapter.

    Get a "Me Account" (a bank account outside of joint finances with husband or other party).

Make some of your own money.

Open a savings account and make a commitment to put a certain amount in it weekly or monthly.

Choose a financial goal and start saving toward it.

Create an agreement with your spouse regarding having your own money.

Develop marketable skills toward a job.

Look for a job.

Consult a financial advisor.

Open an IRA.

Pay bills as soon as they come in.

Balance your checkbook regularly.

Keep track of what you spend every day.

Make a commitment not to use credit cards.

Pay off your credit card balances every month.

Pay down your debt a certain amount every week or month.

Contribute a certain amount to your retirement fund every year.

Make a commitment not to use overdraft protection, except in an emergency. (In this case, make a list of what you consider an emergency, and make a commitment to stick to that list and only that list.)

Give up excuses for spending on things that aren't important.

Buy something for yourself every month as a pure celebration of YOU.

Make a commitment to no longer shop as a way to avoid your feelings.

Add your own statements of financial control:

_____

_____

_____

_____

_____

2.   Review your answers in Exercises #20 and #21 in Step Seven. Are there any more ideas for your one powerful financial decision there? If so, add them to your list of possibilities. Later in the chapter, you'll explore even more ideas to choose from for your one powerful decision.

3.   Of the possible decisions you've written down so far, choose at least two of them, and let's play a "reverse what if" game. This time, instead of catastrophizing, let's think of all the great things that could happen as a result of the decision. For example, "What if I open an IRA and am able to save the maximum allowed every year so that I have more than enough money for retirement?" Doesn't that sound like fun? It will put a positive spin on the actions you might take.

Intuition, Self-Trust, and Self-Respect

When it comes to making choices, Penny's good at trusting her gut. "I made two very powerful financial decisions back-to-back last spring. They both scared me to death," she says. "The first one was saying yes to one-on-one coaching with Nancy. The other was, at Nancy's suggestion, signing up for Marie Forleo's B-School to launch my new business. It was counterintuitive to spend that much money on a class that was about making money. There were so many competing needs. How was I going to tell my husband I wanted to spend this much money on myself when we were anticipating a huge increase in our car insurance? Plus, we had one child in college and another getting ready to start. Deep down, though, I just knew the experiences would be life-changing, and they were.

"As a result of working with Nancy, I'm able to more clearly see my triggers and respond to them more appropriately. I'm learning to have fun, to ask for what I want. I'm learning to flow between work and play with more ease, not waiting for the stars to align before I give myself permission to embrace joy. And it's all because I know I'm worthy of it!

"B-School has proved to be amazing. I haven't even finished it yet, and I've already been inspired to pursue what I'm passionate about—a business that's as intuitive to me as breathing. Since this past spring, I've set up all of the legal and financial aspects of my business. It's up and running! Before I even had business cards made, I had a client paying me more than I had ever imagined. In several short months, I've already more than covered the costs of B-School, as well as the legal and insurance costs."

Penny's work on the steps has really paid off for her. Especially her powerful financial decisions—even though she was worried about the amount of money she was spending.

But what if you're not like Penny, who's good at listening to her intuition and going with it, in spite of her fears? What if you have trouble figuring out what your gut is trying to tell you, let alone trusting it? Making financial decisions can be very scary to many of us, as you saw in my story at the top of the chapter—and as you may know all too well from your own experience. It brings up all sorts of fears, beliefs, and excuses. We frequently second-guess ourselves. We wonder if we're making the right choice. We think, "What do I know about finance?" We have really frightening "what ifs" like mine: "What if I lose everything?"

Increasing your self-worth also means increasing your self-trust and your self-respect. As you've cleared your "operating system" of many of your shadow beliefs, excuses, and underlying commitments, you may have noticed that you have a clearer channel to your intuition and gut instincts. But again, our fears are tenacious, and they're likely to get louder whenever we try to step outside our comfort zone. They can easily drown out our intuition.

First and foremost, if you don't have enough information to know if your decision is a good one, find out! The more you learn about a particular situation, the more you'll trust your decision-making ability.

It also helps to get quiet through meditation. Breathe deeply until you begin to relax and hopefully quiet down the fearful voices in your mind. Then, ask yourself, "What's the best choice for me?" It helps if you have a couple of options to choose from. You can assign each one a number and ask for the right number to pop into your head when you ask the question. Sometimes, the number will pop into your head *before* you even ask the question!

If you still find it hard to make a decision, give it some time. Ask for the answer to come to you in a dream or in a message at an unexpected moment. You could see a sign somewhere, or someone could suggest a book title that makes you think of the right choice.

You can ask others for advice, too, but be careful. Make sure they aren't coming from a place of fear!

Meanwhile, there are ways to boost your self-trust and self-respect as you grow your self-worth. In fact, here's an exercise for exactly that.

EXERCISE #23: SELF-TRUST AND SELF-RESPECT

This exercise is designed to help you recall why you deserve more of your self-trust and self-respect.

1. As we've discussed in previous chapters, we have a tendency to focus on the times when we've made mistakes rather than the times we've had success. If you're experiencing a lack of self-trust and self-respect, it's probably because you're focused on your mistakes. So, for this exercise, make a list of all the times you made good decisions in your life. To help you remember them, answer these questions, and write down what comes to mind as you take yourself back through the years.

   What decisions have you made in regard to jobs and business that have turned out well?

   What decisions have you made in regard to relationships and friendships that have turned out well?

What decisions have you made in regard to money matters that have turned out well?

What decisions have you made in regard to your family that have turned out well?

What decisions have you made in regard to your personal development that have turned out well? (Reading this book might be one of them—I hope!)

2. Keep this list handy for the times when you start to doubt yourself. Add to it every time you make a successful decision, and build on the list to help you maintain confidence in yourself.

Make It a Pattern Interrupt

Before we move on to the final choice of your life-changing decision, there's one important condition to consider: Make sure the decision is not a "normal" move for you. It doesn't have to be huge, but make it bold. It needs to be impactful enough to stretch you a little. I call this a "pattern interrupt"—a way to alter your normal patterns and handle a financial situation in a new way. For example . . .

- If you tend to hoard money like I did, a bold financial move would be to spend some of that money on something that will impact your life.

- If you're used to spending on everyone but yourself, your decision might be to go out and buy something totally pleasurable—just for you.

- If your habit is to overspend, you may decide to cut up a credit card and delete the card data from your favorite shopping websites and online browser autofill settings. Or you could make a commitment to yourself that you won't buy anything but necessities for the next 30 days.

- If you're being supported by someone and want to make your own money, try taking a class to learn new skills, designing a website for yourself (I like the ease and simplicity of Squarespace.com), or creating a product and putting it up for sale on Etsy or eBay.

Through my work with clients, I've discovered five especially popular categories of powerful decisions: (1) hiring someone, (2) spending money, (3) saving money, (4) making money, and (5) handling money better. There are endless possibilities beyond these categories, but let's dive into these five to give you even more ideas for your bold move.

Once you're finished, you'll choose two of these categories to explore—the two that give you the most pattern interrupt for your buck.

Powerful Decision #1: Hire Someone to Help You

Was consulting a financial advisor one of your ways to regain control of your purse strings? If not, you might consider it. We often think it's not worth spending money on financial advice. As you've learned from my experience, it's worth every penny! But be careful whose advice you take. Choose someone who has no stake in your money, and pay the person you hire a fee rather than a percentage. If someone has any stake in your funds, they might be prone to give you less than objective advice. Paying a fee rather than a percentage also protects you from getting stuck with an unexpected bill that feels too high.

In order to take best advantage of the help you get, I encourage you to spend some time learning about the financial world before you hire a consultant. I'm not an expert on the ins and outs of the financial game, which is why this book doesn't cover things like assets, retirement funds, and the like. But understanding that terrain is an important part of your financial self-education. It will also help you feel more comfortable with any advice you receive. While you won't know as much as the professional you hire (or else you wouldn't need them!), you *will* be in a better position to tell if the advice you're being given makes sense. Then, that pesky problem with self-trust won't be such an issue.

There are other hires besides financial advice that you might make as well. If you're getting a new business up and running, you may want to find an hourly VA (virtual assistant) to take care of some of the administrative work for you. Perhaps what you need is an on-location personal assistant to do the same thing for various aspects of your life. Neither of these hires will be terribly expensive, but they can do wonders in terms of freeing up your time. The same goes for hiring someone to clean, garden, or even cook for you—like I did! Such expenses may seem luxurious, but if they're at all within your budget, consider them an investment in a more abundant future.

Powerful Decision #2: Spend Some Money

Those of you who are naturally spenders can skip over this category! This particular pattern interrupt is for those of us who, ahem, have been known to hoard cash out of fear of going without. The defining feature of this category is to spend only the money you *have*. If you'd have to dip into credit, this is not the pattern interrupt for you!

But there are some hoarders out there—I know you, because I *was* you. One of the most powerful financial decisions I ever made was to buy my way out of some of the negative emotion that came with my lousy divorce settlement. Every time it came time to pay the mortgage on the condo my ex-husband was living in, I was filled with resentment. It just felt awful, and I had to go through it every month! But two years into the process, my sister suggested I pay off the rest of the payments in one lump sum. That way, she reasoned, I would never have to write another check. That stopped me in my tracks. On the one hand, why hadn't I thought of that before? On the other hand, I had ten more payments to make, which was no small chunk of change. I had the money in the bank (it was some of the frozen food I'd been planting), but I was also scared. What if I *needed* that money in the next year?

I took a deep breath and realized that I had to pay it in the next year one way or the other. I might lose a little bit of interest by paying it in advance, but what was that compared to all the peace of mind I would gain? I called the bank and asked if there was a penalty for paying it off all at once, and there wasn't. So I did it—and I've never felt so free.

Again, if you're accustomed to spending money on others, it's time to embrace the fact that you're worthy enough to spend money on yourself. This one big decision could turn the tide. If you're afraid of swinging the pendulum too far and starting to spend compulsively, ask a supportive friend to be your safety net. Make an agreement to celebrate with her each time you make a freeing purchase. But at the same time, ask her to reflect back to you if your spending starts to feel reckless.

Powerful Decision #3: Save Some Money

If you're living paycheck to paycheck, have more debt than you want to admit, or just know that money burns a hole in your pocket, this one's for you. The simplest financial decision for spendthrifts is to "buy" into a 401(k) or savings account each week or month. Treat it like a purchase you're making or a regular bill you're paying, and imagine what that savings might allow in your life in the future.

If you truly feel like you don't have enough money to save, start small—set up an automatic transfer of $20 a week from your checking account to a high-yield savings account. (A favorite of mine is 360 Savings from Capital One 360.) No matter how little we have coming in, most of us can afford $20 a week. Over time, that $20 will add up.

The simple act of changing your behavior even a little bit opens up some energy around your finances. You may find that you become more abundant very quickly, allowing you to increase that transfer to $50 or $75 per week in a matter of months.

One of the excuses I hear a lot from overspenders is that they can't save for retirement because they're saving all their money for their child's college tuition. Suze Orman says something on this subject that surprises many people: *"You do a disservice to your children if you pay for their college instead of investing in your retirement."* If you have no retirement fund, the burden will be on them to care for you down the road.

If you truly don't believe you can save any money, look at areas where you might be overspending. Simplifying your lifestyle a bit might actually feel liberating, especially if you tend to live beyond your means. Like Sally, who decided to stop spending $100 a month on her fake nails, you may uncover an unnecessary expense or two. Can you pass on that daily visit to Starbucks, for example? You might feel more empowered if you place that money into a savings account instead.

"Found" Money

There are ways to "find" money for saving. Here are some ideas:

Call your credit card companies, and ask them to lower your interest rates, or transfer balances to lower interest cards.

Always return items that you don't need or want. Don't allow yourself to keep something you won't use, just because it's inconvenient or uncomfortable to get your money back.

Do you have any unused gift cards stuck away in a drawer? Make use of them to purchase birthday or holiday gifts that would otherwise cost you precious dollars.

Always bill right away for services rendered. Do you have any outstanding bills that haven't been paid to you?

Check if there is any money owed to you from people who borrowed from you, and make sure you don't have any unclaimed funds waiting for you at USA.gov.

Look through your things, and see if there are items you don't need. If so, you could sell them on eBay or Craigslist, or have a yard sale.

Check to see if you're overpaying for services like utilities, telephone, television, and Internet services. Are there other companies with better deals?

Do you have any automatic debits and memberships that automatically renew monthly or annually? Don't just let them accrue without deciding if you really need the product or service they're paying for. If you don't use it, lose it!

Powerful Decision #4: Make Some Money

Emily hasn't been in the workforce for 15 years, so she lives in fear that her husband will leave her. Like so many of the women profiled in this book, she doesn't know what she'd do if she had to provide for herself.

If you haven't worked in a long time, or if you're in a low-paying job that you hate, make the powerful decision to get the training required to change your circumstances. Don't tell yourself that it will take too long. Even if you have to go slow, the sooner you start, the faster you'll have the skills you need.

If you don't *have* to work right now because your financial needs are taken care of, still consider getting a part-time job. The benefits of working extend beyond contributing to the household funds. You'll have something more recent on your résumé, you'll feel more confident, and you'll gain experience that will help you feel more secure. You might want to start by researching promising careers for those returning to the marketplace. There's even something called a "Returnship"— an internship for people returning to the work force after a gap of time. It has been a springboard for some people to gain more recent experience and become more marketable.

Have you always wanted to start your own business? There's no time like the present to look into what you'd need to make it happen. A great first step to propel you forward is just to buy the website address you'd want for your business. With the Internet, it's never been easier to sell services or products. You can start with very little money up front.

Remember Sheila who was afraid to ask for money for her intention bracelets? Well, her self-worth has increased so much that she now has a completed website with her entire line of products. Another client, Dara, started her own decluttering business and is experiencing a lot of success. Noele started a coaching business, and she has developed a brand that's already attracting clients.

What would be the most exciting way for you to make more money? Start with one step, but dream big.

Powerful Decision #5: Handle Your Money Better

Several of the choices in Exercise #22 involve getting hold of your purse strings by becoming a better money manager. Do you have trouble facing the truth about your finances? Do you put your head in the sand? If so, *your* best pattern-interrupt financial decision might have to do with changing your behavior around money.

That's what Darlene did. She'd avoided filing her taxes for several years because she just didn't want to deal with it. When she finally took care of it, she had to spend two weeks pulling together all of her records and receipts. Then, she had to face owing a big tax bill, including penalties for not filing on time. It was a harsh lesson, and it was difficult for Darlene not to beat herself up about it.

But after that experience, she was resolved. "It taught me that I want to be a grown up about it now. I never want to have to go through piles of receipts ever again! It was awful!" she says. Now, she's getting software to help her keep track of her accounts, including her deductions. The software will help her balance her checkbook every month, and she'll record all of her expenditures in it weekly. Then, come tax time, all she'll have to do is print out totals for each deduction category, and she'll be ready to go. "What a relief that'll be!" Darlene says. "I already feel my self-worth has increased, just knowing that I'm doing this for myself and not acting in an immature way about my taxes anymore."

Borrowing some of the actions from Exercise #22, here are some of the ways that you might change how you handle your finances:

1.   Pay bills as soon as they come in.

2.   Balance your checkbook every month.

3.   Pay off your credit card balances every month.

4.   Pay down your debt a certain amount every week or month.

5.   Keep track of what you spend every day and how you spend it. Watch for ways to spend more on what you want and less on wasteful items.

6.   Make a commitment not to use your credit cards or bank overdraft protection—except in a true emergency. Make a list of what constitutes an emergency (and be strict) so that you don't stray.

7.   Make a commitment to no longer shop as a way of avoiding your feelings.

8.   Give up your excuses for spending on things that aren't important.

Can you think of other behaviors that would help you manage your money better?

EXERCISE #24: YOUR "ONE THING" LIST

In this exercise, you'll make a list of possible choices for your one powerful financial decision. Then, you'll make your final choice.

1. Choose the two powerful pattern-interrupt categories that make the most sense to you. For example, if you tend to hoard money, you need to spend some of it. If you're an overspender, try saving.

2. Take a look at the list of possible powerful decisions that you wrote for Exercise #22. Which ones are in the pattern-interrupt categories you chose?

3. For each of your pattern-interrupt categories, choose three to five decisions that you could make your "one thing." Get ideas from your Exercise #22 list, as well as from the examples in this chapter. What could you do that's the opposite or different from what you normally do?

4. Take some time to look at each choice and make sure it represents a single step. Don't choose, "Start a new business." You can't do that tomorrow. You *can*, however, buy a URL for your new business or sign up for a course in marketing or website design that will help you move toward launching your business.

5. Write down the decisions you've made. Here's an idea for each of the five categories:

Hire someone to help you:

Example: Hire someone to clean once a week or once a month.

1. _____

2. _____

3. _____

4. _____

5. _____

Spend some money:

Example: Spend $1,000 from savings account on a vacation.

1. _____

2. _____

3. _____

4. _____

5. _____

Save some money:

Example: Commit to saving $100 a month in a high-interest savings account.

1. _____

2. _____

3. _____

4. _____

5. _____

Make some money:

Example: Take an online course in website design.

1. _____

2. _____

3. _____

4. _____

5. _____

Handle money better:

Example: Invest in software to keep track of bank and credit card accounts.

1. _____

2. _____

3. _____

4. _____

5. _____

6. Now, review your possible choices. Which ones make you feel excited? Which ones feel scary? If you're feeling anxiety about taking action, choose the least scary of the decisions on your list. Just take a small step at first that's digestible to you. You don't have to jump from A to Z. If, on the other hand, you feel ready for a bold move, choose something that challenges and scares you a little.

7. Choose something that will serve your future vision rather than your old beliefs—a new commitment replacing an underlying commitment. What new

perspective, new perception, or new choice can you implement today?

8. You don't have to make your choice right this minute, but don't procrastinate. If you want more time, set a nonnegotiable date to make your choice before the week is over. Then, take action on your one powerful financial decision right away. Again, don't procrastinate!

9. After you've chosen your one powerful financial decision, let's not stop there. Choose two or three more decisions that you feel excited about but not quite ready to do. Write them down.

10. For the next financial decision on your list, ask yourself, "What's one new belief that I can input into my operating system in order to move toward acting on this decision?" Write down the new belief, and keep it in a place where you'll see it often.

11. Next, set a deadline to execute this second decision. (If you feel ambitious, go for a third!)

12. Then, as you make your first powerful financial change, prepare yourself for making your impossible desires a reality.

Affirm Your Worth

"The decisions I make move me toward a bright financial future."

UNCOVER YOUR DESIRES—FINANCIAL AND OTHERWISE

Back when I was married, I didn't know what it meant to want anything for myself. I lived in reaction to the needs and wants of others—namely my husband and my colleagues—rather than my own. I was in touch with what I could give others, but I had no idea what my own desires were.

It took working the steps in my previous book and the steps you're reading here for me to even get in touch with what I wanted—just for me. When I first connected with my desires, they seemed crazy and selfish. I thought they were over the top and in some cases even a waste of money. But slowly, I expanded what I thought was possible for me and allowed myself to have more of what I desired. I started to see that some of my desires weren't so crazy after all—I just had to take my head out of the sand. Then, I could give myself permission to want beyond what I thought was possible.

The process culminated in hiring a woman to come to my home in Boulder once a week and cook healthy food for me (as I mentioned in the last chapter). I'd been traveling a lot and all too often would arrive home after a long trip to an empty kitchen. Also I hated to cook, so I'd either grab something quick to eat . . . or just not eat at all. Having this wonderful personal chef fill my fridge during that time was a fabulous convenience since the food she made was ready for me to heat and serve.

I also discovered that it wasn't that much more expensive than going to the grocery and buying food to make myself. So why did it feel like such an extravagance? Just because of my mind-set. The idea of having a personal chef always seemed like something only the very wealthy would do. But my mind-set had nothing to do with reality. Not only was a chef within the realm of possibility, but within the realm of practicality and reason. Still, it took some work to get to a place where I believed I was worthy of paying someone to cook for me, as opposed to simply opening a can of soup.

Once I stopped traveling as much for my job, I had more time to cook for myself and actually found some joy in it. So I decided not to have the professional cook anymore. But I will hire one again in a heartbeat when I feel like it because I've expanded what I think I'm worthy of having.

That experience made me realize that pieces of my desired life are attainable much sooner than I thought. I'm living proof that you can absolutely increase what you believe is possible for you to have!

But first, like me, you have to figure out what your desires *are*. Even after my clients have worked on becoming willing to be worthy, many of them still ask the question, *worthy of what?* It's true that "What do I want?" can be one of the hardest questions to answer—especially for women.

That's why our next step is *Uncover Your Desires— Financial and Otherwise.*

And hey, even if you feel you know full well what you want, I'll bet you can expand your desires even further. This chapter will help you do that, too!

"Desire" Is Not a Dirty Word

Why is it so hard for many of us to know what we want? Often, it's because we get caught up in the fear that we can't have what we want, so why bother? We think it will be too painful to want something that we're convinced we could never have. Then once we do get in touch with a desire, we tell ourselves all the reasons why we aren't worthy of it, why we can't have it, or why everyone else is more deserving than we are. Those excuses are all there to keep us from actually *feeling* desire.

In our culture, we've been told that desire is selfish. If you look at the world as a zero-sum game, then for you to get what *you* want means someone else goes without. But that's not how the universe works. When we receive from an open, honest place, we aren't taking from someone else— we're creating from the abundance that's available to us all. Remember in Step One, we talked about money as energy. And in Step Six, we talked about opening to receive. Creating what we want is just a matter of increasing our self-worth and opening up to the bounty of life. That's true for everybody. When we do that, we're not depriving anyone else.

I also want to make a bold declaration: Having desires doesn't make you a bad person, and it isn't "unspiritual." How do I know? Because *desire is a natural human impulse, and the fulfillment of desire is also natural.* What good is spirituality if it doesn't make room for all of who we are as humans? Living without desire isn't going to work for us. Maybe it's a little easier if you're living in an ashram, isolated from society.

(I don't think so, but since I haven't tried it, we'll allow for the possibility.) Regardless, it's wired into us to strive and want and hope for bigger and better things.

Now, I'm not just talking about wanting objects like cars and houses and jewelry for the sake of accumulating "stuff." I'm talking about a better quality of life, one in which abundance flows freely *to* you and *from* you. I'm talking about a way of life that allows your glass to be full and then overflow in generosity to others—both in terms of your finances and in terms of the qualities you want to receive and express in your life.

But this chapter isn't about giving to others. You'll get to that later. First, you have to become more comfortable with desiring for *yourself*. You have to fill your own pitcher before you have anything to give. For now, allow yourself to marinate in the feeling of wanting. Let it be okay to have desires just for you—because in truth, you absolutely deserve them.

Greed vs. Desire

Buddhism teaches that we're better off not desiring, that we need to just accept "what is." But why can't we accept "what is," while also striving for something more?

When a Buddhist's body becomes hungry, he or she eats. When the body becomes tired, Buddhists sleep. They also desire enlightenment. Buddhism doesn't say there's anything wrong with making a living, either, or buying what we need for food and shelter. So giving up desire entirely is just not possible in the human experience.

What we're most afraid of when we think about desire is actually greed. If you look up the words "greed" and "desire" in the dictionary, you'll see that they have different meanings. A desire is something we wish for. Greed, on the other hand, is defined as selfishness and as *excessive* desire for more than is needed.

Greed is a fear-based emotion. It comes from the belief that there isn't enough, so we need more and more in order to feel safe.

Desire comes from a place of believing that there is plenty, so we can have what we want without any need to be excessive.

Unfortunately, we have a belief in our culture that giving in to desire means we'll become greedy desire machines—that we might become so addicted to our desires that we just take, take, take. But isn't that fear irrational? Yes, there are greedy people in the world, but what's the likelihood that you'll go out of control and become someone you're not just because you allow yourself to *feel* desire? The fact that you're reading a book like this right now, and developing a higher level of consciousness in the process, makes it highly unlikely that you'll turn into a monster just by giving yourself the freedom to *want*.

So if the fear of becoming greedy rears its ugly head, remind yourself of who you are. I'll bet you're someone who loves to give to others. That isn't going to change just because you let yourself have more. In fact, with your own needs and wants taken care of, you're likely to feel even more generous toward others!

The 50 Desires

When my clients get to this step, I ask them to write a list of 50 desires. The list can include desires that cost money and desires that have nothing to do with money. The idea is to let the mind fly without censoring. I ask them to make a list of the numbers 1 to 50 and not get up from their seat until they've written a desire next to each number. And I ask them to encompass the tiny wants, as well as the huge and deep ones. I even suggest they give in to some frivolous wants. The only rule is that only five on the list of 50 can be altruistic desires for other people. Everything else has to be for the self.

Many of my clients have reported that writing their list was more difficult than they expected. Some of them had a hard time keeping their altruistic desires at just five, and others found that it was difficult to separate what they wanted for themselves from what others want *for* them.

That was the case for Carla. She admits that her conditioning has been to "want what everybody else has wanted for me." She has also been conditioned to want for other people but not for herself. So she says, "I started out slowly, desiring things for other people on the top of my list." Then, she wrote her list "unabashedly" without any expectation that any of her own desires would come to pass. It's been 12 weeks since she wrote the list, and already, 18 of her desires have come true or are in progress. For example, she self-published a book that she'd written, and she's gone on more than one trip with her girlfriends. These are just two of the desires on her list that have come to fruition.

When she saw that boosting her self-worth made a difference in her ability to make her desires real, the experience only increased her self-worth further. Each time we create something great for ourselves, we feel worthy of more. It's a wonderful circle that builds on itself and affects every aspect of our lives. "I find myself making health a priority now because I realized that an unhealthy lifestyle didn't fit with any of my desires," Carla says. "I've been taking a lot of vacations—all spontaneous. I'm really conscious of who I share time with—people who are either like-minded or who support my dreams or make me laugh. I'm so unwilling to give time anywhere else. I'm so much happier with the awareness of my goals and desires written down in black and white. It was like a light that had been dimmed has started to shine. They remind me every day what I'm showing up for. I'm an absolute believer that once you do this exercise, there's no turning away from your desires. They become tattooed on your heart and soul."

Here are some of the desires from my other clients' lists:

Desires that cost money or involve career:

1. To buy new furniture for my home.

2. To be debt-free.

3. To have my whole house cleaned weekly.

4. To get a weekly massage.

5. To have an emergency fund of six months' living expenses.

6. To start my own business.

7. To travel to Italy for one month in style.

8. To have a home office.

9. To walk into an Audi dealership and buy a new car with cash.

10. To have a personal trainer.

Personal desires you can't buy:

1. To be at my healthiest weight with no stress about keeping it off.

2. To have balance in my life and work.

3. To allow myself the freedom to do things without expectation of perfectionism!

4. To do what energizes me and let go of what drains me.

5. To have a loving partner to share travel and adventure with.

6. To be energized by my work every day.

7. To have a close network of friends I socialize with.

8. To be hugged every day by someone who's genuinely happy that I'm here.

9. To release and forgive everyone so that my heart is free to bloom into life.

10. To be active and physically fit and want to work out some way every day.

Some desires for others:

1. To take our parents on a wonderful trip, with all of us kids and grandkids, for their 50th wedding anniversary.

2. To help my sponsored child in Armenia, who is now eight years old, with advanced education in some way.

3. To support other women in their growth through nurturing and enlightening workshops.

4. To pay off my sister's mortgage.

5. To finance an after-school arts program.

Now that you have some examples to help spark your own desires, let's try writing your list. For this book, I'm changing the exercise a little bit from how I usually handle it with my clients. For now, we're going to start with just the first 25 of your 50 desires. You'll write the next 25 after the following section. Are you ready? Do you have some desires in mind?

EXERCISE #25: START YOUR 50 DESIRES LIST

This is the beginning of your 50 Desires List, starting with the first 25. For now, don't allow your mind to become bogged down with how you will make any of your desires happen. Too often, we overwhelm ourselves with thoughts like "I could never get this, so I won't even think about it." We don't allow ourselves to dream without the logistics or implementation plan already in place. So please don't worry about logistics yet! Just begin to name—and claim for yourself—what it is that you want.

1.   Write the numbers 1 to 25 on paper, in your journal, or in a document on your computer/tablet.

2.   Don't get up from your seat until you've written a desire next to each number! Let them come to you spontaneously. Remember: Allow your desires to encompass the tiny to the huge, the deep, and the frivolous.

3.   Be sure to write only 5 "altruistic" desires for other people. This is 5 total on your full list of 50!

4.   If you have trouble coming up with your desires, ask yourself these questions:

     What parts of my life would I like to be different?

     What material items would be pleasurable to have around?

     What experiences would I love to have?

What did I dream about when I was a child?

Have I envied what other people have? If so, what have I envied and why? Do I want to put it on my list?

Think Beyond Your Means

As we talked about in Step Six—Become Willing to Be Worthy—once you begin to let yourself *want*, it's important to expand what you believe you deserve and can have. In other words, begin to *think beyond your means.* I'm not suggesting that you *live* beyond your means! That's a totally different thing. Living beyond our means is a rebellious reaction to the fear that we don't have enough. For example, we tell ourselves that we're too poor to have what we want, and the next thing we know, we're running off and buying something we can't afford because we feel so deprived.

On the contrary, *thinking* beyond our means can be a remedy for deprivation, and actually prevent overspending. As we allow ourselves to desire more (while we continue working with our limiting beliefs, excuses, and underlying commitments), we expand what we believe is possible for us.

Nearly all of us have a ceiling on what we believe we can get in life. We think, "I get this much, but no more." It's like animals in zoos who get used to small cages. Even when placed in large habitats, they sometimes stay in an area the size of their former cage. They become accustomed to their limitations and don't feel comfortable with more.

A study with goldfish is a case in point. The fish were raised on one side of a big aquarium that had been divided into two sections by a clear wall. When they tried to swim to the other side of the aquarium, they bumped into the wall. After a few months, the researchers removed the wall, but the goldfish never tried to swim beyond where the wall had been. They had learned their lesson well: Trying to swim "over there" would be painful! So they remained imprisoned by their own choice.

We're no different. Based on past experiences and fears of the unknown, we put ourselves on a starvation diet that restricts us from experiencing as much pleasure and joy as we're capable of. Even if we *can* imagine something more, it often feels like a fairy tale—totally out of reach. But the ceiling that we create for ourselves is a result of our limiting beliefs, nothing else.

Why are we so much more comfortable thinking about what we *can't* have, and why we can't have it, than we are thinking about what we *could* have? Once again, it feels safer. If we don't go for what we want, we can stay safe and small on the familiar side of the aquarium. We don't have to risk failure or disappointment. We don't have to risk the possibility of finding out that we aren't as worthy as we'd hoped. That's an irrational fear, of course, because as we've already clarified, we're worthy just by the fact that we're alive!

It's a fear I know far too well. I was the kind of person who woke up each morning and thought, "What do I have to worry about today?" Now, thanks to the process in this book, I rarely worry at all.

There's also this weird truth, which is that we kind of love to complain. We get off on staying in our suffering space. Feeling deprived and restricted not only helps us feel safe, but it also gives us an excuse to gain sympathy. For many of us, sympathy feels like love. Have you ever competed with someone about which of you had it the *worst*? It's hard to understand why anybody would want to win a contest like that, but in an odd way, it makes us feel special. For that reason, "I've suffered more than you" becomes a mantra—you're surely familiar with some people like that. But of course, such a mantra keeps us in a small enclosure, in only half of the aquarium. And it prevents us from allowing our desires to become reality.

The only way out of that small space is to let your desires run free!

Lucky for us, we can become aware of the limitations we've put in place. Once we see them, we can use our imaginations to *think beyond them.* Just by being willing to imagine the "impossible," we're swimming past the invisible wall and into a more expansive future.

When my clients make their 50 Desires Lists, I ask them to allow some of their desires to be outlandish, over the top, or even impossible in their estimation. Of course, those are just value judgments. Many of my clients' so-called outlandish desires have come true. Often, the impossible can become possible—when we let it.

Here are some of the more outlandish or lofty desires that my clients put on their desires lists:

1. To spend time with Richard Branson.

2. To win a Grammy . . . or five!

3. To receive compensation of $150,000 or more for one speech.

4. To write a *New York Times* best-selling book that gets translated into 20 or more languages.

5. To be cast in a Broadway musical.

6. To have a few viral videos and a large Internet following.

7. To spend at least 25 percent of my time working on my art.

8. To give a TED Talk that goes viral.

9. To own several homes around the world.

10. To buy an island, name it after my daughter, and share it with her.

Do those "impossible" desires give you any ideas? Let's write your remaining 25 desires while you think beyond your means. How can you further expand what you believe is possible for you to have?

EXERCISE #26: TOP OFF YOUR 50 DESIRES LIST

This time, you'll complete your list of 50 desires with your second 25. Remember to think beyond your means, and let your mind go wild!

1. Write the numbers 26 to 50 on a piece of paper, in your journal, or in a document on your computer/tablet.

2. Don't get up from your seat until you've written a desire next to each number! As you think beyond your means, don't make up lofty desires just for the sake of it. Get in touch with the "outlandish" desires that truly excite you, and write them down.

3. Again, remember no more than 5 altruistic desires for other people! This is 5 total on your full list of 50. If you've already written 5 desires for other people in your first 25, don't include any more here.

4. Once you've completed the list, go back through all 50 desires. Next to each one, write the *feeling or experience* you believe having that desire will bring you. It might be comfort, joy, fun, beauty, security, safety, or any number of feelings. As it turns out, desire isn't so much about the "having" of the item or experience, but rather the *feeling* it will bring you.

5. Take a look at your full list from 1 to 50, and let yourself marinate in your desires. What does it feel like? How many of your desires feel outrageous or impossible? Take note because I'll bet many of them will feel a lot more possible—very soon!

Getting a Bigger Plate

Suze Orman says that if your life's outgrowing your plate, get a bigger plate. Many of us live with a mind-set of deprivation because the plate we hold for ourselves is too small. Then, there's Cheryl Richardson, who says that a high quality life has more to do with what you subtract than what you add.

It may sound like they're contradicting each other, but they're actually saying the same thing. In order to have what we desire, we have to "get a bigger plate," as Suze says. And sometimes, to make room for what we want, we have to subtract what no longer serves us.

Cheryl's point is that many of us accumulate "stuff" and things to do to try to fulfill ourselves in a false way. We might do that because we haven't stopped to think about what we really want. Or because we don't think we're *worthy* of what we really want. By subtracting, we make space for what we *truly* desire. So the first step is to eliminate the things we don't want. We've already begun that process by eliminating the obstacles of shadow beliefs, excuses, and underlying commitments. We may also have physical things to eliminate in order to make room for what we want. Or we may feel that some relationships no longer serve us.

Then, getting a bigger plate is all about expanding our self-worth. By following these steps, you're doing just that. By accepting your worthiness, you'll become capable of increasing your capacity to have what you want in life.

Now, it's important to note that when Suze talks about the bigger plate, she's not talking about getting more stuff. Once again, I want to be clear that I'm not just talking about material things. As my client Ellen says, "If I don't care about me enough to honor myself and my own needs, it doesn't matter if I'm worth a billion dollars on paper because the money will be useless."

It's absolutely true that money can't buy happiness, but it *can* buy you a certain amount of comfort, in a variety of different forms. And there's nothing wrong with that! Money can reduce external stresses, even as you work on increasing your self-worth from the inside. In other words, there's nothing wrong with having creature comforts and beautiful things. We don't have to suffer in order to be worthy. We're meant to have a good time as often as we can! As the ancient Sufi poet Rumi wrote, "The soul is here for its own joy."

What I'm advocating isn't magical thinking or manifesting. I'm simply suggesting that you give yourself *permission to want*. All you need to do is see that it's possible to have more than you've been letting yourself have. When you do, your potential will simultaneously, automatically begin to increase. The old adage "I have to see it to believe it" has the whole thing turned around. In truth, we have *to believe it to see it* in our lives. As William Blake said, "What is now proved was once only imagined."

So flex your dreaming and visioning muscles, and see how big a plate you can allow on your table! As my clients and I have proven, you *can* turn your desires into your day-to-day life.

EXERCISE #27: TAKE ACTION TOWARD YOUR DESIRES

Let's work with some of the desires you wrote in your list of 50 so that they become part of your reality, and no longer desires at all.

1. Look at your 50 Desires List, and choose the top 5 that you feel are the most attainable. For each of these desires, write down your answers to the following questions:

   "Is there anything I have to eliminate from my life to have this?"

   "What resources do I have now that would help me attain this desire?"

   "Is there someone I could ask for help?"

   "What's one action I can take toward making this desire real—even if it's just to look at the fears, beliefs, excuses, and underlying commitments that might be in my way? What self-worth exercise from Step Six could I repeat to help me get closer to the fulfillment of this desire?"

2. Pick one of your "lofty" desires that you feel might be unattainable, and answer these questions about that desire:

"What would I have to eliminate from my life to have this? What obstacles are in my way?"

"What resources do I have now that would help me attain this desire?"

"Is there someone I could ask for help?"

"What's one action I could take toward this desire, even if it's just to look at the fears, beliefs, excuses, and underlying commitments that might be in my way? What self-worth exercise from Step Six could I repeat to help me get closer to the fulfillment of this desire?"

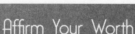

Affirm Your Worth

"My desires are not just possible, but probable."

GET READY TO DO
THE IMPOSSIBLE

"I was living like a vagabond. Like a complete vagabond," Noele says of her apartment situation when she first started working the steps in this book. "I spent so many years feeling like I didn't have a way to live better, to have my own living space without roommate situations, many of which were horrific." But as her self-worth increased, Noele wasn't willing to continue living like a vagabond. She *was* willing to be worthy, though. So, she found a place of her very own.

"I make enough money to maintain my monthly bills, but it was the moving costs and the furniture and all of that. They were above my present income. It wasn't such a risk that I was putting myself in danger, but I was definitely stretching as far as I could," Noele says. Part of her development has been to launch a side hustle—her own coaching business—while she continues in a full-time job. Just when she was afraid she wouldn't have the money for furniture and moving costs, a new client came along with a payment that covered everything.

"It helped me see that it isn't impossible for me to live the way I want to live or to create whatever it is I want to create," Noele says. "The furniture is paid for, all the extra costs to turn utilities on—all that's covered. And it wasn't as hard as I expected it to be. I'm just really excited and still observing a little in disbelief. This work has really shifted things. There was a huge gap between my desires list and how I was living. For years, I couldn't live according to my worth. To no longer be in that space—and so quickly? It feels great!"

When each of my clients wrote down their list of 50 desires, almost all said that many of the items felt like impossible dreams. Yet after just a few weeks of working these ten steps, quite a few of those "impossible" desires were already a reality or well on their way. And these results are consistent across the board! There's no reason why the same can't happen for you. That's why Step Ten—your last step in this process—is *Get Ready to Do the Impossible*!

I'm not promising miracles here. I've seen significant movement and positive change in everyone who has worked through this process. Including myself!

Once you've done the internal work to feel worthy of wealth and joy, the possibilities expand outward into every area of your life. You've already heard my story about doing what I thought was impossible—paying off my mortgage; quitting my job; becoming a full-time coach, speaker, and author . . . just to name a few. Not long ago, I never would have dreamed that I could be doing what I love most—and making more money than I made in my full-time job! But here I am. It's my life!

The same is true for Marlene. She longed to be a full-time writer for years, but put it off due to insecurity. She was using the excuse that she didn't know how to become a writer. After dipping her toe in freelance writing on the side while working in an office job, she discovered that she could get enough work to sustain herself full-time. It was still scary to quit her job and take the leap. But today, she's just surpassed her ten-year anniversary as a full-time freelance writer. "I still can't believe this worked," she says. "I really did think it was impossible for me, and I've proven myself so wrong. I love my life!"

Marcy thought it was impossible for her to become a Certified EFT (Emotional Freedom Technique) practitioner, and within 12 weeks of working these steps and growing her self-worth, she was able to do it. Now, she already has some paying clients.

Christina started helping people declutter on the side, and the next thing she knew, she had a moneymaking business. "I can't believe I'm sitting here with a business that I'm ready to give birth to," she says. "I always thought, 'What do I have to offer? Doesn't everybody know how to organize their stuff?' But no, they don't. They need help. And sometimes, it's just about holding their hand. I have a man paying me good money now to help him get organized. I could be at work in his house for the entire summer."

Amy says that these 8 items from her list of 50 have already come true, so she has checked them off as "done." "Many of these were lifelong or ongoing desires," she says.

1. Have a fulfilling, mutually rewarding, and loving marriage free from score-keeping. √

2. Make my plan, then work my plan every day. √

3. Support women who are truly changing lives and nurturing others to live their life purposes. √

4. Spend two weeks with my brother and his family each year. √

5. Spend two weeks with my parents each year. √

6. Go on one girls' night out each month. √

7. Go away for a girls' weekend once per year. √

8. Spend quality time with my dog every day. √

Now that money and shadow beliefs are no longer your convenient excuse for not following your heart, what do you want to do?

As poet Mary Oliver asks, *"Tell me, what is it you plan to do with your one wild and precious life?"*

Chloe's Story

"There have been many changes in my life since I started doing this work with Nancy. Our lease was recently up on our car, and my husband and I felt we were in a place to buy something. It just so happened to be around the time of my birthday, and I've always wanted a Lexus 350. We agreed that we would buy a used one and that our budget was around $25,000. We were initially going to pay cash so that we would have no monthly payments. In the past, I would defer to whatever my husband thought was best, but this time, I suggested we speak to our financial advisor. It turned out that by rearranging a few things and financing the car, we would end up paying significantly less over the course of the five-year loan.

"I was much more involved in the discussion and even came up with a number of scenarios to consider before we made our decision. Because of the savings, we felt comfortable buying a more expensive and newer model. It's perfect, and I feel very empowered that I was an equal partner in the process.

"Another example is that I'm partnering with a woman who's a fitness expert and founder of a juice company. In the past, I would be really into the creative process but not that into discussing finances and business. This time, I brought up the subject, and she agreed that it would make sense to have all the business aspects agreed upon up front. She's a single mom, and I know she works really hard. For a brief second, I heard myself think, 'I don't need to get paid as much as she does.' Then, I breathed and said, 'We will both be paid equally, fairly, and abundantly.' I reminded myself of all my hard work, past and present, and feel good about moving forward in a financially proactive and professional way."

Living Wealthy

My perfectionism and my history—the pain I experienced around my brother's death when I was so young—turned me into someone who didn't know how to play or relax. In fact, I was so concerned about spending *any* time not working that I frequently worked during my off hours while I was at Hay House. It made no sense, of course, since I had a set salary. I would make just as much if I relaxed and enjoyed my time off as if I spent it crouched over my computer. But I wasn't thinking logically! My beliefs told me that if I wasn't working, I wasn't valuable. And if I wasn't valuable, I wasn't safe.

It wasn't until I left my job and started working for myself that I began to give myself time to play and enjoy my life. Which is ironic, since as any entrepreneur knows, when you're working for yourself, there's no such thing as paid time off! But my self-worth was finally intact, and I no longer believed I had to be a workhorse to validate my value. After that shift, I not only began to make more while working fewer hours, but I also began to learn how to enjoy my downtime. I can now play and relax without feelings of fear or guilt!

You, too, can surprise yourself with what you can create in your life. Like Chloe and so many of my clients, Keira has done just that: For several months now, she's maintained a higher bank balance by herself than she ever had when she was with her husband. And that's happened simply because she was willing to let go of her dependency on him and try to make it on her own. She proved to herself that what she thought was impossible was indeed possible.

Another of my clients has already, in a short period of time, paid down her debt by nearly 98 percent. Another held her breath and raised her rates in her professional life—only to discover her clients were perfectly willing to pay more for the valuable service she offers. *What can you do to surprise yourself?*

As you continue to do the internal belief work required to increase your sense of self-worth, you'll find you can suddenly tolerate and allow more—more money, more time, more love. You'll find that there's room for everything you need in your life—family, relationships, the right kind of work, and playtime. Now, that's *true wealth*! That's when the impossible becomes possible.

EXERCISE #28: DREAM THE IMPOSSIBLE DREAM

What's the biggest dream you can come up with? Let's take a more careful look at your 50 Desires List and expand on it.

1. Review your 50 Desires List from Exercises #25 and #26 in Step Nine. Place a check mark by the ones that feel impossible to you.

2. Are there any bigger, more expansive desires you'd like to add to your list? Can you take your desires up yet another notch? For example, I got to a point where hiring a personal chef was definitely in my list of possibilities, while having a private jet still feels a bit impossible to me—though it sounds awfully nice considering how much I travel! Don't hold back. Let your imagination

run wild! Here are some other examples of these kinds of "no holds barred" desires:

Becoming a billionaire

Driving a Tesla Model S

Living in Hawaii

Hiring a private driver and personal chef

Starring in a movie

Backpacking across the Sahara

Owning a helicopter

3. Of the desires you've written down, which one is your biggest dream? (If you want to write more than one, please do!) Can you become willing for these impossibilities to become possible?

The Impossible Is Coming!

As you work toward increasing your self-worth and allowing more wealth to come into your life, be patient. Your inner work on your beliefs, excuses, and commitments will pay off step by step. The impossible is coming—but don't expect it to arrive overnight. Some of your desires will probably happen quickly and easily, while others will require more time.

If you find yourself feeling antsy, practice positive self-talk to keep your outlook bright and forward thinking. Let's say you dislike your job, and you're working on your self-worth so you can leave it and start your own business. In the meantime, you're taking courses and learning new skills. But it's still too soon. You can't leave the job yet, and it's frustrating. Each day, you can remind yourself, "This job is supporting me while I work toward a better future. I'll be there before I know it."

Continue to create new beliefs to replace old limiting beliefs. For example, if you find yourself thinking, "I'll never get out of this job," change that to "I know I'm worthy of doing the work that I love," or "I'm capable of running my own successful business."

Even if you still feel far from where you'd like to be, remind yourself that each powerful financial decision is like planting a seed. Over time, they can't help but grow into a bountiful garden. Each step you take is in support of allowing in the "impossible." Each step gets you closer to the future you're imagining for yourself. You're making an investment in the life you envision—one choice at a time. And if you make a choice that doesn't work out, learn from it and let it go. Beating ourselves up is another tactic we use to stay small. Simply brush yourself off, and make another powerful decision. The impossible may lie behind the very next door you dare to open.

Let Your Cup Run Over

Now that you've opened your channel to receive so much more, you have much more to give. When you fill your own pitcher first, it can't help but overflow into the lives of those you love and care about. Once you're full, you're able to give with a full heart. Giving out of obligation, habit, or false beliefs will be a thing of the past.

Here's an example from my own life. A friend and coaching colleague called me and said that her niece, who is in her early 20s, had a lot of the same issues that I had in my past—perfectionism, people-pleasing, and the fear of letting people see my flaws. "I would love to gift her coaching sessions with you," she told me. "What would you charge?"

"I would love to do this for you pro bono," I answered. "I love the idea of working with someone so young. We can dismantle her patterns before it's too late!"

"I can't let you do that," my friend said. "I have to give you something in exchange."

"Okay, I'm going to do ten sessions with your niece. You send me a check for whatever feels right to you."

My friend ended up sending me $1,000. What did I do? I donated it to *my* niece's fund-raising initiative. She crafts flowers out of brightly colored duct tape and attaches them to the end of pens. She then sells her creations as "Petals for Parkinson's." All proceeds go to research for Parkinson's disease.

It was quite remarkable how good I felt after making that donation. It was a completely different feeling from the one I got when I bought gifts for my husband. Back then I was buying for him so he wouldn't leave me or be angry. This time, I gave from a place of pure love—with no price tag. I expected nothing in return, and I didn't need to prove anything with my generosity. When we have enough for ourselves, it just feels good to give to others.

EXERCISE #29: GIVING BACK

Let's explore how you can begin to give back.

1. What would you want to give if you had all the money and time in the world? Make a list of what you would do or create or donate. Here are some ideas:

   Donate money to start a school or orphanage.

   Found my own charity for a cause that's close to my heart.

   See to it that an animal shelter on the verge of closing stays open.

   Spend several months volunteering in a village in Africa or Asia.

2. Maybe you don't have the money *right now* to do something as big as start your own charity, but you never know what your future holds. Meanwhile, what are some altruistic moves you could make right now? Here are some ideas:

   Devote time to working with the elderly in the community.

   Sponsor a child, woman, or family in need.

   Research charities with causes that have meaning for me, checking their reputation to make sure the funds would be used properly, and commit to making regular (monthly or quarterly) donations within my budget.

   Volunteer to work with kids or prison inmates, or to build houses for Habitat for Humanity.

My Wish for You

Movement mobilizes possibility, and change begins with making a different choice. Take one powerful action, and everything will begin to shift and crack open.

My hope is that, with the information you've read in these pages and the insight you've gathered from the exercises you've completed, you're already creating that shift and starting to own your worthiness.

Remember, we choose our limits based on what we believe we're worthy of having. My wish for you is that the "I am not enough" belief has dissolved and transformed into "I am capable and deserving of everything I desire."

Please also remember to be gentle with yourself. Acknowledge the inner critic and turn her volume down as you continue taking risks and building your courage muscles. Explore your 50 Desires . . . and then create 50 more.

My desire is that you will know that you are deserving of love, fulfillment, and richness . . . regardless of what you do or don't do. That when you let go of the labels you applied to yourself in the past, you'll see and know that you have always been whole.

May these words and experiences open your heart and mind to having all that you desire. May the impossible cease to exist for you.

And may you know, always, that you are worthy.

Affirm Your Worth

"I have enough because I know I am enough. I am worthy."

APPENDIX

Resources

Barbara Stanny's *Overcoming Underearning*

Kate Northrup's *Money: A Love Story*

Suze Orman's Must Have Documents: http://www.suzeorman.com/books-kits/collections-and-kits/must-have-documents/

Financial Advisor Melissa Sweet: www.melissasweetmoney.com

Alexis Neely's Money Map: http://www.moneymap.tv

Mint software: https://www.mint.com

Quicken software: http://www.quicken.com

QuickBooks software: http://www.quickbooks.intuit.com

Virtual assistants: http://www.assistu.com

Helpers around the house: http://www.taskrabbit.com

Cleaning service: http://www.merrymaids.com

The Ford Institute for Transformational Training: http://www.thefordinstitute.com

The Shadow Process: http://www.thefordinstitute.com/shadowprocess

Team Northrup: www.teamnorthrup.com

ACKNOWLEDGMENTS

"Thank you" just doesn't cut it. I'm beyond grateful for the limitless love and support of so many.

Louise Hay: For teaching me how to *be*.

Reid Tracy: For being my greatest cheerleader and most trusted advisor, and for helping me realize a life beyond my dreams.

Debbie Ford: For the great honor of carrying your legacy forward.

Doreen Virtue: For being my sacred sister on the way to worthiness.

Melanie Votaw: For the elegant brilliance with which you breathe life into my voice on the page.

My "Worthy Girls": For your transparency, devotion, enthusiasm, and faith. This book wouldn't be what it is without you.

My coaching clients: For trusting me to guide and witness you.

Margarete Nielsen and Mollie Langer: For helping me make a seamless transition. I treasure our friendship.

Diane Hill, Richelle Fredson, Sally Mason, Charles McStravick, and the whole Hay House team: For making sure this book has exactly what it needs to impact as many people as possible.

Diane Ray, Mike Joseph, Steve Morris, Rocky George, and the whole Hay House Radio crew: Thank you for making *Jump Start Your Life* such a joy each week and helping me shine.

Amy Kazor, Pat Denzer, Kathy Henry, Terry Nolan: For being my phenomenal team behind the scenes. I appreciate each of you so much.

Julie Stroud (my secret weapon), Kelley Kosow, Fran Fusco, The Ford Institute and my fellow coaches: For being family.

Maria Bailey, Colette Baron-Reid, Gabby Bernstein, Kris Carr, Heather Dane, Arielle Ford, Melissa Grace, Ahlea Khadro, Gail Larsen, Bill Miles, Kristen Noel, Christiane Northrup, Kate Northrup, Suze Orman, Nick Ortner, Daniel Peralta, and Cheryl Richardson: With much love for the singular role each of you plays.

Patty Gift: For your inspired edit, wisdom, grace, and effortless companionship . . . you are a fabulous worthiness mentor.

Kelly Notaras: For your limitless devotion to me, this project, and to us. You will forever be my NSLP.

Aaron Thomas: For your love and willingness.

Mom and Dad: For everything. Really.

Kate: For being the other half of my heartbeat . . . and for sharing Allan, Isabel, and Simon with me.

ABOUT THE AUTHOR

Nancy Levin, best-selling author of *Jump . . . And Your Life Will Appear* and *Writing for My Life,* is a Master Integrative Coach and the creator of the JUMP Coaching and WORTHY Coaching Programs, working with clients—privately and in groups—to design lives in alignment with their own truth and desires. She was the event director at Hay House for 12 years and hosts her own weekly call-in show, *Jump Start Your Life,* on Hay House Radio. Nancy received her MFA in Creative Writing and Poetics from Naropa University in Boulder, Colorado, and she continues to live in the Rocky Mountains. You can visit her online at www.nancylevin.com.

౿ HAY HOUSE TITLES OF RELATED INTEREST ౨

YOU CAN HEAL YOUR LIFE, the movie, starring Louise Hay & Friends
(available as a 1-DVD program and an expanded 2-DVD set)
Watch the trailer at: www.LouiseHayMovie.com

THE SHIFT, the movie,
starring Dr. Wayne W. Dyer
(available as a 1-DVD program and an expanded 2-DVD set)
Watch the trailer at: www.DyerMovie.com

HOW TO LOVE YOURSELF (AND SOMETIMES OTHER PEOPLE):
Spiritual Advice for Modern Relationships,
by Lodro Rinzler and Meggan Watterson

LIFE LOVES YOU: 7 Spiritual Practices to Heal Your Life,
by Louise Hay and Robert Holden

MIRACLES NOW: 108 Life-Changing Tools for Less Stress, More Flow,
and Finding Your True Purpose, by Gabrielle Bernstein

MONEY, A LOVE STORY: Untangle Your Financial Woes and
Create the Life You Really Want, by Kate Northrup

MONEY, AND THE LAW OF ATTRACTION: Learning to Attract Wealth,
Health, and Happiness, by Esther and Jerry Hicks

YOU CAN CREATE AN EXCEPTIONAL LIFE,
by Louise Hay and Cheryl Richardson

All of the above are available at your local bookstore,
or may be ordered by contacting Hay House (see next page).

We hope you enjoyed this Hay House book. If you'd like
to receive our online catalog featuring additional information
on Hay House books and products, or if you'd like to find out more
about the Hay Foundation, please contact:

Hay House, Inc., P.O. Box 5100, Carlsbad, CA 92018-5100
(760) 431-7695 or (800) 654-5126
(760) 431-6948 (fax) or (800) 650-5115 (fax)
www.hayhouse.com® • www.hayfoundation.org

Published and distributed in Australia by: Hay House Australia Pty. Ltd.,
18/36 Ralph St., Alexandria NSW 2015 • *Phone:* 612-9669-4299
Fax: 612-9669-4144 • www.hayhouse.com.au

Published and distributed in the United Kingdom by: Hay House UK, Ltd.,
Astley House, 33 Notting Hill Gate, London W11 3JQ
Phone: 44-20-3675-2450 • *Fax:* 44-20-3675-2451 • www.hayhouse.co.uk

Published and distributed in the Republic of South Africa by: Hay House SA
(Pty), Ltd., P.O. Box 990, Witkoppen 2068 • info@hayhouse.co.za

Published in India by: Hay House Publishers India, Muskaan Complex, Plot
No. 3, B-2, Vasant Kunj, New Delhi 110 070 • *Phone:* 91-11-4176-1620
Fax: 91-11-4176-1630 • www.hayhouse.co.in

Distributed in Canada by: Raincoast Books, 2440 Viking Way, Richmond,
B.C. V6V 1N2 • *Phone:* 1-800-663-5714 • *Fax:* 1-800-565-3770
www.raincoast.com

Take Your Soul on a Vacation

Visit www.HealYourLife.com® to regroup, recharge,
and reconnect with your own magnificence.
Featuring blogs, mind-body-spirit news, and
life-changing wisdom from Louise Hay and friends.

Visit www.HealYourLife.com today!

READY TO RECLAIM YOUR WORTH?

Join My Next Worthy Coaching Group!

Worthy Coaching provides a proven process for dissolving the underlying emotional, psychological, and spiritual roadblocks, clearing the path for wholeness, fulfillment, and richness in all areas of your life, not just your bank account.

I am here to ensure that you create deep and lasting change. Let me support you in taking powerful, consistent, accountable action toward the life you most desire, on the solid foundation of knowing your own value and worth.

Take the first step in moving from where you are to where you want to be right now!

To express my gratitude to you for purchasing this book, I'm gifting you savings on an upcoming Worthy Coaching Group. Please visit: www.nancylevin.com/worthycoaching/ and enter the code MYWORTH to receive your $100 discount.

Due to the nature of this work, I only coach a handful of clients one-on-one at a time. If you feel private coaching is right for you, please reach out to me via my website.

. . . .

Click . . . And Your Coach Will Appear!

www.nancylevin.com

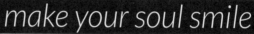